I HAVE A VOICE!

My Journey of Faith from Victim to Victor

Barbara A. Walker

I HAVE A VOICE!
ISBN 13: 978-0-9910427-0-8
ISBN-10: 0991042700

Copyright © 2013
Barbara A. Walker
All Rights Reserved

Unless otherwise noted, all Scripture quotations are from the New King James Version of the Bible.

For more information or to order additional books, please submit $17.95 (which includes the cost of postage) to:

Barbara A. Walker
377 North Commerce Street
Aurora, Illinois 60504
w.o.e.word@godswomenofexcellence.com
www.godswomenofexcellence.com

Published by Barbara A. Walker

Printed in the USA by
CreateSpace
4900 LaCross Road
North Charleston, SC 29406

DEDICATIONS

This book is dedicated to my wonderful family! What a blessing they have been to me. Through all my messes and mess-ups, they have always loved me unconditionally. I thank and praise God for the richness of His blessing upon us.

In loving memory to my mom, Pearlie Mae Lee Jackson, who was the wind beneath my wings and my biggest cheerleader. Right, wrong, or indifferent, she had my back. And, in memory of my brother, Hardis Lee Jackson, Jr. (JR). R.I.H.

To my dad, Mr. Hardis Lee Jackson, Sr., and the coolest siblings – ever: Jennifer, Cedric, Kimberly, Gewanda, Valerie, Martin, Tracey, and Michael.

To God's greatest gift to me in my beautiful children: Antonio, Bernadette, Eric, and Shamica, and the most amazing grandchildren I could have ever had, even if I had hand-picked them: Devonte, Trestin, TaeShaun, Aniya, Tyler, and Anthony, Jr.

The Lord our God is an awesome God. I want to thank and praise Him for all of His wondrous blessings upon my life!

<u>*My Declaration of Praise*</u>

*1: I will bless the Lord at all times; His praise shall
continually be in my mouth.
2: My soul shall make its boast in the Lord;
the humble shall hear of it and be glad.
3: Oh, magnify the Lord with me, and let us exalt His name together.
8: Oh, taste and see that the Lord is good;
blessed is the man who trusts in Him!*
Psalm 34

I Have a Voice!

I am a professional woman who holds an MBA in Business Management and multiple industry-specific designations. I manage a team of other professionals and **DAILY** make decisions which place millions of dollars of my company's assets on the line. I am actively involved in my church, teaching others about living the abundant life, equipping and empowering women through my local church as well as district and state associations, serving on the Prayer and Hospitality Ministries. I am a published author and provide daily encouragement via my W.O.E. (Women of Excellence) Word devotionals. I am a mother and a grandmother, a sister, an aunt, and a daughter. And for more than 15 years, I was the victim of domestic violence.

I thank and praise God that I am now educated, equipped, and empowered for *life*. Empowerment refers to increasing the spiritual, political, social, educational, gender, or economic strength of individuals and communities. Regardless of the impetus of our empowerment, it must be internalized to **become** and is evidenced by our confidence and increased awareness of the abilities we possess. Empowering women fuels the driving passion of my life: to share my life experiences for the benefit of others and use them as tools to educate and empower women everywhere. I want to remind women that they have a voice and should rightfully expect to be able to use it.

Domestic violence is anything but empowering. It is a drain on society and is still an unspoken, taboo subject for many of us. Domestic violence and emotional abuse are behaviors used by one person in a relationship to control the other. It is about power and control. It has nothing to do with love or jealousy. **It is all about power and control.** Partners may be married or not married; heterosexual, gay, or lesbian; living together, separated, or dating.

Domestic violence and abuse can happen to anyone, yet the problem is often overlooked, excused, or denied. This is especially true when the abuse is psychological, rather than physical. Noticing and acknowledging the signs of an abusive relationship is the first step to ending it. No one should live in fear of the person they love. If you recognize yourself or someone you know in the following warning signs and descriptions of abuse, **SPEAK UP**! You have a voice – use it. There is help available, therefore, there is hope.

Examples of abuse include:

- name-calling or putdowns
- keeping a partner from contacting their family or friends
- controlling or withholding money, even taking your paycheck
- stopping a partner from getting or keeping a job
- actual or threatened physical harm to you, your children, or other family members
- threatening suicide to get you to do something
- forcing you to have sex or to do sexual acts you do not want or like
- stalking
- intimidation

Violence can be criminal and includes physical assault (hitting, pushing, shoving, etc.), sexual abuse (unwanted or forced sexual activity), and stalking. Although emotional, psychological, and financial abuse are not criminal behaviors, they **are** forms of abuse and can lead to criminal violence.

The violence takes many forms and can happen all the time or once in a while. An important step to help yourself or someone you know in preventing or stopping violence is recognizing the warning signs. But let you in on a little secret – for me, there were no warning signs. It was often when I thought things were well, when I wasn't "on guard" that he would snap about something that really had nothing to do with anything. If I spoke to the wrong person, if I didn't answer the way he wanted me to, if I "breathed" (or so it seemed at times) – anything was enough to set him off. Slapping. Punching. Beating with a stick or belt. Black eyes. Bloody noses. Then he got "smart" and start doing things which still left me battered and bruised, but hidden by my clothes so that others couldn't see them.

There are some common myths associated with domestic violence. Here are a few:

- **Domestic violence is not a problem in MY community.**
- **Domestic violence only happens to poor women and women of color.**
  - Domestic violence happens in all kinds of families and relationships. Persons of any class, culture, religion, sexual orientation, marital status, age, and sex can be victims or perpetrators of domestic violence.
- Some people deserve to be hit. All I can say to that is – **REALLY?!?!?**
- Alcohol, drug abuse, stress, and mental illness cause domestic violence.
- Domestic violence is a personal problem between a husband and a wife.
- If it were that bad, she would just leave. **You have no idea!**

A victim can be defined as:
- a person who has been attacked, injured, robbed, or killed by someone else
- a person who is cheated or fooled by someone else
- someone or something that is harmed by an unpleasant event

I've often asked myself "How did that happen to me? How did I become a "victim"? How did someone who felt that her whole life was an adventure to be discovered wind up becoming a victim and another statistic?" Eleanor Roosevelt said, *"Remember, no one can make you feel inferior without your consent."* And I said, 'humph!'

I can tell you **what** happened, but I cannot fully explain **how** it happened. The truth is **I-do-not-know**! It started subtly but quickly escalated. We lived 20 hours away from my family, so I was literally cut off from any support. By the time we moved closer, the mind-numbing isolation was already done! *"It's hard to fight an enemy who has outposts in your head."* (Sally Kempton) During those early years, he had managed to change me from the **ME** that I knew and loved into the **HER** I still don't recognize, even when looking back. Little comments and put downs. Threats and big moves, but no actual blows. Until...

Women too often suffer in silence. We spend a lot of our time nurturing others, yet are left feeling unloved. We take care of our homes and those in it, but often have to fend for ourselves when we need care. More and more women are raising children single-handed, whether they be single moms, divorced moms, or widowed moms. We work all day and come home to work some more. We women are phenomenal, but after all these years, many women still have to be reminded that we have a voice.

My abuse was no different than a lot of other women in the way it was perpetrated. As is fairly common, it started with words; it was verbal, emotional, and psychological. "Nobody will ever love you but me", "you are worthless", "you are ugly", and "you are so stupid" were just a few of the things I heard on a regular basis. It was an attack on my identity. I heard these words so much that I started believing them. As I accepted his abuse, desperately trying to avoid anything that might set him off, I lost myself and forgot who I was. In a short amount of time, he completely isolated me from my family and made sure I had no real friends. He took away what self-esteem I thought I had and turned me into a scared, weak, lying woman who was afraid to do what she knew she had to do. But one day, I realized that I had a voice, and it would be silenced no longer.

> I LEARNED THE HARD WAY THAT I CAN'T ALWAYS COUNT ON OTHERS TO RESPECT MY FEELINGS, EVEN WHEN I RESPECT THEIRS. BEING A GOOD PERSON TO OTHERS WILL NOT ALWAYS RESULT IN THEM RETURNING THAT GOODNESS BACK TO YOU. YOU CAN ONLY CONTROL THE THINGS YOU DO AND ALLOW YOUR ACTIONS AND WORDS TO SPEAK VOLUMES ABOUT THE TYPE OF PERSON YOU ARE. AS FOR THE PEOPLE IN YOUR LIFE, YOU MUST CHOOSE TO ACCEPT THEM FOR WHO THEY ARE OR CHOOSE TO WALK AWAY.
>
> http://www.daveswordsofwisdom.com/2013_09_01_archive.html

Albert Camus said, *"Nothing is more despicable than respect based on fear."* You cannot force a person to respect you, because respect is earned. But because most abusers are fear-filled themselves, they use force and violence in their misguided efforts to force you to respect them, to love them, and to recognize them in whatever role they may have in your life.

I don't blame him – I allowed it to happen. I said it was to protect my children from the stigma of growing up in a broken home. I told myself that it was to "save face" among my church brothers and sisters. But the truth is, I gave up my identity in search of becoming who and what I thought I was supposed to be. Alice Walker said, *"The most common way people give up their power is by thinking they don't have any."* The first time he hit me should have been the last time he hit me. The first time he verbally abused me should have been the last time he said something hateful to me. But I took it because I thought that was what a woman was expected to do. I took it because I thought that in order to appear happy, I needed to be tied to a man with a home and a family. I took it because I had not yet learned who I really was. Today, I know who I am. I have a voice, and I have a story to tell.

> **NEVER BE BULLIED INTO SILENCE. NEVER ALLOW YOURSELF TO BE MADE A VICTIM. ACCEPT NO ONE'S DEFINITION OF YOUR LIFE, BUT DEFINE YOURSELF.**
> (Harvey Fierstein)

Audre Lorde, a Caribbean-American writer and civil rights activist, wrote in *"Sister Outsider: Essays and Speeches"*, *"Your silence will not protect you."* She was so very right! My silence was **his** shield. It protected **him**. It gave **him** a public image which was nothing like his private one. I covered for him. I lied for him. I helped him perpetrate his façade. In many ways, I did it for myself. I was so confused, ashamed, and afraid that what he was saying about me was true. And I was ashamed and afraid of what others would think of me if they knew. I felt helpless and hopeless.

I was caught in a trap of my own making. I wasn't the perpetrator, but I was the enabler. Every time he beat me and I pretended that everything was alright, I was making it easy for him to do it again. Every time he belittled me and I tried to make him love me, I was providing validation to him that he was right about me.

"Everything in your life is there as a vehicle for your transformation. Use it!" (Ram Dass). I endured years of poverty, more years of physical, emotional, and mental abuse, followed by a year of sickness and disease just to be able to say that there is nothing in your past which cannot be used to help you walk into your destiny. **NOTHING!** It doesn't matter what that may have been. *That* is your past. Your future and your destiny are ahead of you. I **was** a victim, but today, I **am** a victor! I am one who faced my enemy and he has been defeated! All it took to win that battle was to remember who I was. Once I did, I was able to walk out of that debasing life and never look back.

Today, I know that I have a voice, and I am determined that it be heard.

- ✓ No more suffering in silence!
- ✓ No more hiding behind a façade, trying to present an image that others wanted to see!
- ✓ No more shame and guilt over something which I did not do!

When I left, I was terrified. But I was free! God gave me the faith I needed to trust Him completely. I didn't know how things would turn out, but I knew that they would be better than they were. I had family all around me, but my children and I moved into a shelter because I was that afraid of what would happen next. He had me convinced that he would kill me if I ever left him. So every time I went to work, every time the door of the church opened and someone entered, every time I stepped outside, I expected to die. But I had decided that I would rather die *free in my spirit* than spend one more minute in the hell I was in. I had decided that it was time that I begin to live my life.

I had come into the knowledge that I had a voice, and I **WOULD** be heard.

When it comes to domestic violence, silence is a woman's worst choice. It leaves her vulnerable and exposed. She has no witnesses in the event of escalation. She has no one looking out for her to be sure she is okay. She has no one, and that puts her abuser in a position of power.

"Forgive people in your life, even those who are not sorry for their actions. Holding on to anger only hurts you, not them."[1] Our life experiences can make us bitter or they can make us better. I chose the better. I thank God that I don't look like what I've been through! Know this: there is nothing that we **were** which cannot be used by God to shape us into who He knows **we will be**. We are being changed into His image, moving from ***glory to glory***, day by day. He will accomplish His will in us and through us, **by any means necessary!**

> **I CAN BE CHANGED BY WHAT HAPPENS TO ME,**
> **BUT I REFUSE TO BE REDUCED BY IT.**
> Maya Angelou

The last stanza of Maya Angelou's poem *I Know Why The Caged Bird Sings* reads:

> **The caged bird sings**
> **with a fearful trill**
> **of things unknown**
> **but longed for still**
> **and his tune is heard**
> **on the distant hill**
> **for the caged bird**
> **sings of freedom.**

---

[1] http://www.daveswordsofwisdom.com/2013/07/holding-on-to-anger-hurts-you.html

One day I heard the voice of God, and I remembered that I had a voice, and it was time that it my voice be heard. I refused to live the same way any longer, caged by the fear of what would be. Walking out of that abusive relationship, speaking up about it, and standing up for myself – facing my fears head-on without regard for the consequences – set me free and gave me the strength that I needed to live my life God's way – whole, healthy, and loving myself. I have always had a voice, but for too long, it was silent. I **do** have a voice – "*CAN YOU HEAR ME NOW?*"

> **WHEN I LOOK BACK ON MY LIFE**
> **I CAN SEE THE PAIN I'VE ENDURED,**
> **THE MISTAKES I'VE MADE, AND**
> **THE HARD TIMES I'VE SUFFERED.**
>
> **WHEN I LOOK IN THE MIRROR,**
> **I SEE HOW STRONG I'VE BECOME,**
> **THE LES SONS I'VE LEARNED, AND**
> **I'M PROUD OF WHO I AM.**
>
> www.daveswordsofwisdom.com

DO YOU NEED HELP? IT IS AVAILABLE. IF YOU DO NOT FEEL SAFE, YOU NEED TO GET HELP IMMEDIATELY!
IN THE AURORA, IL AREA, YOU CAN CALL:

MUTUAL GROUND (A SHELTER IN THE STORM)
(630) 897-0080 24/7 HOTLINE FOR DOMESTIC ABUSE
(630) 897-8383 24/7HOTLINE FOR SEXUAL ASSAULT

INTRODUCTION

Life is so good. I didn't always know that. I spent the first thirty-five years of my life searching for what I already had. I made a lot of bad choices in life, looking for love in all the wrong places. It is my prayer that you will avoid some of the pitfalls of my life, clearly seeing the warning signs and moving around them. I wish someone had cared enough to tell me what I am sharing with you. If only...

****

I thought I had won! After all, he had chosen me. All the women in the community were throwing themselves after him. But somehow, he picked me out of the crowd. Twenty and single with two small children. Unattractively underweight. Seemingly confident yet continually seeking validation. He picked **me**!

When he asked me to move to New York with him, I thought I had died and gone to heaven. In a short amount of time, I quit my job, sold my furniture, and prepared to "fly away" with my prince charming. *"What about my children? I want to bring them with me"*, I asked. *"Let's get you settled in first; we'll send for them in a couple of months,"* he promised. And naïve little girl that I was, I believed him. But that one lie was the first of many and the beginning of my more than fifteen-year nightmare with the man of my dreams.

Growing up in the South, I dreamed what most girls dreamed. I would meet the right man, get married, have two children, and live happily ever after. Yea, I dreamed of college. At one point, I really wanted to be a school teacher. Other times, my vision was of being a nurse. (These were the only professionals to which I was exposed, so that was the limit of my aspirations.) I was a good student, and I knew that my only real hope of college would be scholarships and grants. With my parents' limited income and the number of children in the house, that should not have been an obstacle. All I had to do was stay focused in school and I would get there.

But like many childhood dreams, mine became a dream deferred …. until I remembered – **I HAVE A VOICE!**

****

THE FUTURE BELONGS TO THOSE WHO BELIEVE IN THE BEAUTY OF THEIR DREAMS.
Eleanor Roosevelt

**WHAT A WONDERFUL LIFE I'VE HAD!
I ONLY WISH I'D REALIZED IT SOONER.**
Colette

Chapter 1 ~ The Cycle of Domestic Abuse

Chapter 2 ~ Identity Crisis

Chapter 3 ~ Your Rendezvous with Destiny

Chapter 4 ~ Identity Check

Chapter 5 ~ I AM

Chapter 6 – Facing Your Fears

Chapter 7 ~ I AM ~ Really!

Chapter 8 ~ The Joy of Being a Kept Woman!

Chapter 9 ~ Living with Purpose

Chapter 10 ~ You Are Special to God

Chapter 11 ~ Victorious Living

Chapter 12 ~ Prisoner of Hope

Chapter 13 ~ Triumphant in Spite of My Limp

Chapter 14 ~ Stay in the Fight

Chapter 15 ~ The Journey is the Destination

Chapter 16 ~ A Living Hope

Chapter 17 ~ Breaking Free of Fear

Chapter 18 ~ The Miracle in You

Chapter 19 ~ I'm Brand New!

Chapter 20 ~ My Battle Scars of Victory

Chapter 21 ~ Never Give Up!

Chapter 22 ~ Renew Your Mind

Chapter 23 ~ Now Live – Victoriously!

Chapter 24 ~ The Power of One Voice

Chapter 1 ~ The Cycle of Violence in Domestic Abuse[i]

**YOU MAY BE DISAPPOINTED IF YOU FAIL,
BUT YOU ARE DOOMED IF YOU DON'T TRY.**
(Beverly Sills)

****

In 70 – 80% of intimate partner homicides, no matter which partner was killed, the man physically abused the woman before the murder.[2]

Domestic abuse falls into a common pattern, or cycle of violence:

---

[2] Campbell, et al. (2003). *"Assessing Risk Factors for Intimate Partner Homicide." Intimate Partner Homicide*, NIJ Journal, 250, 14 – 19. Washington, D.C.: National Institute of Justice, U.S. Department of Justice.

- **Abuse** – Your abusive partner lashes out with aggressive, belittling, or violent behavior. The abuse is a power play designed to show you "who is boss". *I was **never** prepared. No matter what the scenario might be, he would catch me off guard. The cursing and put downs would happen during the abuse, never as a warning that it was coming. And it was always my fault that he hit me – always!*
- **Guilt** – After abusing you, your partner feels guilt, but not over what he's done. He's more worried about the possibility of being caught and facing consequences for his abusive behavior. *He would always be super nice to me afterwards, continually telling me that I **made** him me. He would always say how sorry he was and it would never happen again.*
- **Excuses** – Your abuser rationalizes what he or she has done. The person may come up with a string of excuses or blame you for the abusive behavior – anything to avoid taking responsibility. *It was always my fault. "I didn't respond quickly enough." "I didn't act as though I loved him." "I had a 'bad attitude." "I don't want this for dinner!" "Why can't I find my favorite jeans."*
- **"Normal" behavior** – The abuser does everything he can to regain control and keep the victim in the relationship. He may act as if nothing has happened, or he may turn on the charm. This peaceful honeymoon phase may give the victim hope that the abuser has really changed this time. *This would be the time that he would try to "woo" me – taking me out to dinner, telling me he loved me, asking my opinion about things.*
- **Fantasy and planning** – Your abuser begins to fantasize about abusing you again. He spends a lot of time thinking about what you've done wrong and how he'll make you pay. Then he makes a plan for turning the fantasy of abuse into reality. *This was the part that he was best at – hiding what he was thinking. I wouldn't know until afterwards what had set him off. But it would be clear that he*

had spent time thinking about what he would do to me. I remember once while visiting my parents, I waved to a friend who passed by. (Nothing unusual about that; I'm from the South and you speak to everyone.) A few minutes later, he asked me to go with him to another friend's house. I had no idea what was coming next. He drove me down a dark, narrow path and stopped the car. He didn't slap me or punch me in the face, because he knew we would be going back to my parents. But instead, he took a small branch from a tree and whipped me across my back until it was bloody. When he was finished and saw the mess he had made of my back, he made sure I had a jacket so that no one else could see, then drove us back to my parents as though nothing had happened.

- **Set-up** – Your abuser sets you up and puts his plan in motion, creating a situation where he can justify abusing you. *At one point, we lived in a small apartment without a washer and dryer. I was hand washing some clothes for the children in the bathroom sink. He asked me if he had any clean t-shirts. I responded that I didn't know and he should check in the underwear drawer. The next thing I knew was seeing stars! Before I could turn back to finish what I was doing, he had come into the room and punched me in the mouth for "getting smart with him".*

It's sad, but it is a fact that there is a cycle of domestic abuse. Knowing that should have made me smarter, right? Wrong! Even though there is a cycle, we have to remember that it is coming from a mind which is not logical, and therefore, cannot be predicted with any specificity. That "not knowing" was the merry-go-round of my life for more than fifteen years.

Your abuser's apologies and loving gestures in between the episodes of abuse can make it difficult to leave. He may make you believe that you are the only person who can help him, that things will be different this time, and that he truly loves you. However, the dangers of staying are very real.

There is a definite cycle to the violence of domestic abuse. Don't do what I did and believe the lies that he's sorry and it will never happen again. It will! No matter how you try to trivialize or rationalize it, it is wrong. Before you get in too deep, please, get out! I was blessed to have survived. Not every woman who experienced what I did can say the same thing.

> **Your ambition should be to get as much life out of living as you possibly can, as much enjoyment, as much interest, as much experience, as much understanding. Not simply be what is generally called a "success".**
> Eleanor Roosevelt

Chapter 2 ~ Identity crisis

THE VALUE OF IDENTITY OF COURSE IS SO OFTEN WITH IT COMES PURPOSE.
(Richard R. Grant)

****

Domestic violence is the leading cause of injury to women – more than car accidents, muggings, and rapes combined.[ii]

Identity crisis is an internal conflict of and search for identity. Simply stated, it's when you don't know who you are – really! Yes, you answer to your name. Yes, you have a role to play and you do it to the best of your ability. Yes, you have stuff and things which are associated with who you are. But, deep down, you are always wondering about your real identity. Do I fit in? Am I loved? Does anyone need me? Am I good enough? or pretty enough? or thin enough? or tall enough? Who am I?

Identity crisis, according to psychologist Erik Erikson, is the failure to achieve ego identity during adolescence.[3] During this stage, we are faced with physical growth, sexual maturation, and integrating our ideas of ourselves and about what others think of us. We form our self-image and endure the task of resolving the crisis of our basic ego identity. Successful resolution of the crisis depends on our progress through previous developmental stages, centering on issues such as trust, autonomy, and initiative.

All through scripture, we see God calling people who were suffering from identity crisis. Moses. Abraham. Jacob. Saul/Paul. Peter. Elijah. Naomi. Jeremiah. Then, there is the focus of our thought for today, King Saul. In response to their request, God selected Saul as the first king of His people, Israel. If anyone had reason for confidence, it was Saul. His father was

---

[3] http://en.wikipedia.org/wiki/Identity_crisis

wealthy and influential, and Saul himself had a commanding stature. Saul looked like a king, he was anointed and appointed by God, and should have been a great king. Yet, when Samuel came to appoint him as king, he questioned him, saying that his own family was "the least important of all the families" of Benjamin. He asked Samuel, "Why are you talking like this to me?"

Saul would repeatedly struggle with this sense of inferiority and insecurity, his identity crisis. Throughout his reign, Saul would be obsessed with his fears and his image. Everything he said and did was selfish because he was worried about managing them.[4] His insecurities would eventually cost him his relationship with God. (And, sadly, when God withdrew His Spirit from him, he didn't even know it!)

Although God had called Saul and given him a mission in life, he struggled constantly with jealousy, insecurity, arrogance, impulsiveness, and deceit. He failed to realize that God does not measure men by their wealth, influence, or good looks, but by their hearts (1 Samuel 16:7). He didn't believe that God "lifts the poor from the dust" and "sets them among princes" (1 Samuel 2:8). Saul refused to rest in God's favor, so he constantly tried to prove himself.

I found myself lost within myself during a dark period of my life. When I was in the midst of an abusive relationship with too much fear to walk away, I didn't recognize myself. I played my roles to the best of the ability, and if anyone noticed that something was wrong, they never said. But I was lost and confused. I did not know who I was. More importantly, I didn't know **whose** I was!

Do you know who you are, or are you wrestling with your own identity crisis? How are you trying to prove your worth? Whose standards are you using? (If they are anyone's other than God's,

---

[4] *God's Story for My Life*: Bible Gateway, July 30, 2013

you need to *"consider your ways"*.) Are you competing against someone or comparing yourself to someone other than Jesus? You need to learn what Saul didn't; you need to learn to rest in God's favor.

You need to thank God for the honors He has given you, and not look at your own deficiencies as something which makes you inferior. Thank Him for making you **you** – a citizen of His Kingdom and an heir and joint-heir with Christ. When you remember that, when you rest in the confidence of your place in the Kingdom, it's kind of hard to doubt who you really are.

Father, thank You for making us new creatures in You. Thank You that when You made us new, You also gave us new names, so that our identities are tied directly to You. We can be confident of who we are because we know Whose we are. We are children of the King ~ hallelujah! In Jesus' name. Amen.

****

**LIFE HAS KNOCKED ME DOWN A FEW TIMES.
IT HAS SHOWN ME THINGS I NEVER WANTED TO SEE.
I HAVE EXPERIENCED SADNESS AND FAILURES.
BUT ONE THING FOR SURE ... I ALWAYS GET UP!**

Chapter 3 ~ Your Rendezvous with Destiny

MY FUTURE IS SECURE BECAUSE IT IS IN HIS HANDS.

****

Studies suggest that up to 10 million children witness some form of domestic violence annually.

The 101st Airborne Division – the "Screaming Eagles" – is a U.S. Army modular light infantry division trained for air assault operations. This division's motto is "a rendezvous with destiny". I love that! It makes no difference how many times I hear it, I always come back to the fact that God has a perfect plan for our lives, and no matter what route we take, we must eventually fulfill our destiny. Along the way, we take some detours, go down dead-end streets, down some roads the wrong way, even sometimes running out of gas. Eventually, in spite of it all, we will make it to our destination.

The Screaming Eagles' motto always reminds me that I have a rendezvous with **my** destiny. If I get off track, because of my foolishness or someone else's, I can never forget that I have a rendezvous with **my** destiny. Because the sovereignty of God completely controls my life and everything that affects it, I can be completely confident that I will reach the destiny God has ordained. I may stray off course, but God has a way of getting me back on track, because His plan for my life is perfect and will be fulfilled.

Let me give you an "over-the-top" review of the Biblical story of the four lepers. Their experience took place during a time of famine. Even though it was a terrible period in their lives, and their story is an exciting reminder that God will help to make it us if we start walking by faith. My pastor said that *"the choice is yours, but your choices are determined by the sovereignty of God"*. That is good news!

You see, the lepers were starving outside the city, ostracized because of their condition. One day, they decided that they had to make a choice. Interestingly, every choice before them seemed to lead to death. If they went back into the city, they would die because they would be stoned to death. If they stayed where they were, they would die of starvation. But if they went to the Syrians (the enemy), if they got up and moved forward, they **might** die, or it was possible that the Syrians would have mercy on them and allow them to live.

Once they decided to make a move, God met them at their weakest point. He had already put His plan in motion; the prophet had spoken. But it took the actions of these four dying men, walking toward their destiny, to bring it to pass. The lepers approached the Syrian camp. But rather than hearing the footsteps of four sick and dying men, the Lord magnified the sound. The Syrians thought they heard the sound of an army marching upon them, and they fled, leaving everything they had in the camp. When the lepers got there, they found not just enough for themselves, but enough to feed the Israelites who were shut up in the city because of their fear of the Syrians. Our God is an awesome God! They got up, started walking, and God did the rest. That's my challenge to you today.

If you stay where you are, you will die. *That was the place I was in when I thought I was trapped in my abusive marriage. In my mind, I felt that I would die if I stayed there one more day. It took me a long time, but one day I ran for my life, because I had decided that I would rather die **on my terms** than live that way another day.*

If you go back (to dead relationships, dead-end jobs, and hopeless situations), you will die. *I made the mistake one day of meeting my then-husband to "talk" (or, so he said). He wanted one more chance* *to ask my forgiveness, to convince me that we could work it out. I was free of him, and I had no intention of going back. So what made me agree to meet him, I will never know. Maybe it was Satan's attempt to take me out, because I will never forget the experience – ever! He took me to the apartment where he was living, and this time, I was sure I **would** die. He beat me with his fists, kicked me, punched me in the face, shoved me into walls, and threatened to shoot me (get this) if I didn't take him back. Of all the beatings I had endured from him, this was the worst. I was off work for an entire week, and was still bruised and sore when I returned the following Monday. I wore dark glasses for weeks to cover the bruises on my face. I was silly (once again), but he taught me the best lesson I could ever learn. If I had any doubt, I knew then that I had made the right decision.*

Walk <u>into</u> your destiny; remember – your destiny is NEVER behind you. *The only path to abundant life is straight ahead. Seek the Lord, trust His divine plan, follow His leading, and walk into your destiny. But don't remain selfish. When you find your purpose, when you find the path to your destiny, don't forget your sisters and brothers. Share your blessings, and God will bless you even more. I am a living witness that He has – and He is – doing great things for me!*

Deciding to leave my abuser and put my trust in God was not easy. I didn't know where I would live. I didn't know how other people would see me. I didn't know much of anything except *I wanted to live*, and I couldn't do that as long as I allowed myself to be victimized and trapped.

Father, thank You for preparing a perfect plan for our lives. It is so exciting knowing that You have already laid out our destinies. Our finish is assured because You have ordained it. Knowing that our future is secure in Your hands gives us the hope we need to face each new day. Help us to never forget that You are always working in our lives, gently leading us to the place You have predestined for us. In Jesus' name. Amen.

Chapter 4 ~ Identity Check

**DEFINE YOURSELF RADICALLY AS ONE BELOVED BY GOD.
THIS IS THE TRUE SELF. EVERY OTHER IDENTITY IS ILLUSION.**
(Brennan Manning)

****

Every 9 seconds in the US a woman is assaulted or beaten.

Do you know who you are? Are you sure? It seems like the whole world is suffering from identity crisis. So, do you know who you are? We often identify ourselves by our roles – "I'm Betty's mom", "I'm Johnny's wife", "I am a school teacher", "I am a professional dancer". But is that the real us? When you answer in this way, are you speaking with certainty about who **you** are? Maybe it's time that you do an identity check.

It is sometimes hard for us to separate our "who" from our "do". We identify ourselves with what we do, and forget who we are. We take pride and build our self-worth on other people's opinion of our "do". But what about your "who"? Do you take pride in who you are as a person?

Challenging our identify has been on Satan's agenda since he tempted Eve in the garden. We cannot afford to allow him to distract us. His lies won't change who we are. But they can cause us to act as though we are someone else and thereby miss our blessings. You know how that is. A person who is constantly told they are ugly will believe it unless they have positive affirmations to counter that. A child who is told they are stupid will begin to act stupidly regardless of how smart they may be. A bold, confident woman can be demoralized if she is abused or neglected by someone she cares about. (I can attest to that from personal experience!) So, it is important that you know who you are.

As an abused woman, I didn't know. His continual put downs were so systematic, and so traumatic, that they left me confused. *Could it be that I really was unloveable? Was he the only man who would value me as a woman? Was it possible that I was as stupid as he said? Was I ugly? Was I too thin? Too tall? Incompetent? Irrelevant?* **Were the things that he said about me really true?**

To come into our own, we have to believe that we are who **GOD** says we are! We are children of the King. We are heirs and joint heirs with Christ (Romans 8:17). We are the righteousness of God (II Corinthians 5:21). We are saints in the world (Ephesians 2:19). We are holy (I Peter 1:16) and sanctified (I Corinthians 6:11). We are fearfully and wonderfully made in the image of God (Psalm 139:14), and we are citizens of heaven (Ephesians 2:6). That's who we are! No one can take that away from us. We should not allow anyone to make us think or feel otherwise. No matter what our past sins may have been. No matter what choices we may have made. That was our "do". But God doesn't see us that way. He sees our "who". His vision of us is not limited to the here and now, but He sees us as the glorious creatures we are becoming. Hallelujah!

Father, thank You for Your faithfulness. You are always there for us. When we are walking according to Your will, or even when we veer off the path, You never leave us or forsake us. Thank You, Lord, for being our shepherd and our guide. In Jesus' name. Amen.

TAKE PRIDE IN HOW FAR YOU HAVE COME AND HAVE FAITH IN HOW FAR YOU CAN GO.
Christian Larson

Chapter 5 ~ I AM

> I DO NOT WISH (WOMEN) TO HAVE POWER OVER MEN,
> BUT OVER THEMSELVES.
> (Mary Wollstonecraft)

****

Nearly 1 in 5 teenage girls who have been in a relationship said a boyfriend threatened violence or self-harm if presented with a breakup.

"To be or not to be, that is the question" is a line from "Hamlet" by William Shakespeare. It could mean a lot of different things, but the most commonly accepted meaning of the statement is "Is it better to live or to die?" Hamlet was tormented by the pains of life, yet fearful of the uncertainty of death. So, he questioned his existence. There are times when the connections that come to my mind are nebulous at best, but I thought of this question as I listened to Kirk Franklin's "I Am". Many times, we question our own existence. Maybe not whether we should live or die, but we wonder about our purpose and our reason for being.

God has never wondered about Himself or His creations. He is a very purposeful God, and everything He has created has a distinct purpose in His grand scheme of things. So, when God sent Moses as a deliverer of His children from bondage, He had no problem when they wanted proof that it was really God who had sent him. They had been seeking a deliverer for many years, and they wanted to be sure that Moses was truly an ambassador of the Lord. When Moses objected to going back to Egypt, saying that they would want to know His name as proof of who He was, "*...God said unto Moses, I Am That I Am: and He said, Thus shalt thou say unto the children of Israel, I Am hath sent me unto you.*" (Exodus 3:14). How cool is that??? When asked to prove who you are, you simply reply "I Am"!

Thousands of years later, as Israel again looked to God in hope of the Messiah, Jesus came "...*in the volume of the book* ..." (Hebrews 10:7). He came to fulfill all that had been written about Him by the prophets and in the law. And He, too, came as the great "I Am". Jesus declared of Himself: "... *I am the bread of life* ..." (John 6:35); "...*I am the light of the world:* ..." (John 8:12); "*I am the good shepherd*" (John 10:11); "... *I am the resurrection, and the life* ..." (John 11:25); "... *I am the way, the truth, and the life* ..." (John 14:6); "...*I am Alpha and Omega* ..." (Revelation 21:6). By identifying Himself as "I Am", He associated Himself with Jehovah. By identifying Himself as "I Am", He confirmed Himself as the fulfillment of the promise, just as God had confirmed His identity to Israel while they were in bondage in Egypt.

As children of the most-high God, we also need to know who we are. We cannot declare ourselves to be "I Am", but we can assuredly say, "I am who God says I am". We can say with confidence, "*I am redeemed*", "*I am delivered*", "*I am holy*", "*I am righteous*", "*I am sanctified*", "*I am healed*", "*I am more than a conqueror*", "*I am victrious*". We can say this with unwavering conviction because the great "I Am" has said it, and it is so.

Father, thank You for being the great I Am! Because You are, we are all that You say that we are. Thank You, Lord, for making us new again. In Jesus' name. Amen.

FREEDOM COMES WHEN YOU ACCEPT THE FACT THAT GOD LOVES YOU EXTRAVAGANTLY!
Creflo Dollar

Chapter 6 ~ Facing Your Fears

A WOMAN IS THE FULL CIRCLE. WITHIN HER IS THE POWER
TO CREATE, NURTURE AND TRANSFORM.
Diane Mariechild

Most cases of domestic violence are never reported to the police.[5]

****

When talking about fear, the "super-saint" will say that f.e.a.r. is nothing more than false evidence appearing real. That sounds really spiritual. But when face-to-face with our own fear, it is anything but false evidence! There are some circumstances which scare us. When we encounter those, fear looks mighty real to us. Life happens, and we have to deal with it.

- Called into the boss's office for making that same mistake – again – creates a level of fear. *"Lord, You know I need this job!"*
- Being declared cancer-free, then finding a lump in your breast – creates a level of fear. *"I know God is a healer, but is that His plan for me?"*
- Seeing your loved one struggle with that addiction, even after they have declared *"for God I'll live, and for God I'll die"* – creates a level of fear.
- Feeling that pain in your chest after undergoing the surgery which was supposed to make it all better – creates a level of fear. *"Lord, I need you now!"*
- Sitting by the bedside of your loved one, praying that God will raise them up – creates a level of fear. *"Not my will, but Yours…"*

---

[5] Frieze, I.H., Browne, A. (1989) Violence in Marriage. In L.E. Ohlin & M. H. Tonry (eds.) *Family Violence*. Chicago, IL: University of Chicago Press.

Fear is real. It was not "false evidence appearing real" when I literally ran away from my abuser. It was not unrealistic to expect retaliation for trusting God to deliver me from my desperate situation. My fear was **real**, and I know that it was nothing but the grace of God which gave me the strength to do what I had to do. As quiet as it's kept, we all have that one thing that we fear more than anything. Denying it doesn't make it go away. The only antidote for fear is faith. How do you muster up your faith when faced with the thing that you fear the most? The "super-saint" will say that "Faith is substance of things hoped for, the evidence of things not seen". And it is. Ask them to explain what that means and they can't, (even though it sounds "super-spiritual"!)

The fear was real when I faced my batterer time after time. The fear was even more real when I made up my mind to leave him under the threat of death. But I had the promise of God, and though I was petrified, I believed that my later days would be better than my former.

The believer who is standing on their trust in God will simply declare, "Lord, You did it for me last time, I know You can do it again!" The believer who has walked with God, who has experienced His healing or deliverance or protection or provision or peace or power, the believer who knows that they know the love and power of the living God, will feel fear. There is no shame in that. But when they remember the goodness of the Lord, when they remind themselves of the faithfulness of our God, their faith will give them the strength that is needed in order to walk on, trusting that God will work things out according to His perfect plan. When fear comes, an experienced saint will praise their way through by faith!

Fear is real. It may be based on new encounters. Sickness or disease for that person who has never been sick. An unexpected accident. The loss of a child or a parent. Divorce. Financial bankruptcy. As often as it comes from unexpected things which happen in our lives, fear is often based on past experiences. We groan in our spirits, "Oh, Lord, not again!" But take heart! Real faith – enduring faith – is also based on past experiences. Because of what God did before, we keep walking by our faith which is built upon the hope that we have in God.

Life happens, and we don't always understand why we go through what we go through. There are times that God "turns up the heat" in our lives to deepen our holiness[6]. We may need some heat to melt the wax so the seed can bear the fruit and shape us more into the character of Christ. The fire we experience won't consume us, because God will never put more on us than we are able to bear. But it is intended to make us purer by removing all the barriers hindering us from our growth in Christ. The next time "heat" comes in your life, don't be afraid. Trust that the Lord will use the fire of your sufferings to burn up the bad and make way for the good. Be assured that the day will come when your ashes will be turned into beauty.

Father, thank You for taking us through the purifying fire of Your love and grace. We know You remain faithful in the midst of our trials and will bring us out on the other side for Your radiant glory. Help us to remember that even in the face of fear, You are there with us. Because of You, we are assured victory, even when it looks like we are losing. Thank You, Lord! In Jesus' name. Amen.

GOD WILL NEVER LEAVE YOU EMPTY.
HE WILL REPLACE EVERYTHING YOU LOST.
IF HE ASKS YOU TO PUT SOMETHING DOWN,
IT'S BECAUSE HE WANTS YOU
TO PICK UP SOMETHING GREATER.
Facebook: JCLU Forever

---

[6] Toews, Becky. Power to Change: Out of the Fire. March 30, 2013

Chapter 7 ~ I AM ~ REALLY!

NEVER UNDERESTIMATE THE POWER OF A WOMAN.
Nellie McClung

Domestic violence victims lose nearly 8 million days of paid work per year in the US alone—the equivalent of 32,000 full-time jobs.

****

One of the simplest and most-profound names of God is "I Am". It is the name by which God revealed Himself to Moses. And it is the name by which Jesus confirmed His identity to the Jews. "I Am". It is so simple that its meaning can be missed. And it is so profound that it conveys the fullness of all that God is.

Israel spent 430 years enslaved in Egypt. When God was ready to deliver them, He sent Moses to lead them out. God called Moses from a burning bush. After many objections and excuses, Moses asked God how he should respond when the children of Israel asked, "What is His name?". God's response? "I AM WHO I AM." And He said, "Thus you shall say to the children of Israel, 'I AM has sent me to you.'" (Exodus 3:13b, 14).

In one of Jesus' discussions with the Jews, they questioned His statement regarding Abraham. Jesus responded, "Most assuredly, I say to you, before Abraham was, I AM." (John 8:58). His response made the Jews so angry they wanted to stone Him. They knew that by identifying Himself as "I AM" He was identifying Himself as God. He was not identifying with God; He was saying that He was God.

That's good news for us! We can be assured that have the God of the universe is in control of everything in our lives. Look at how He identified Himself to the Jews. Jesus declared, "I am the bread of life." (John 6:35). The context was the Manna in the wilderness (Exodus 16:13 – 18). By this statement we know it was meant to be a model of the Messiah. Whoever partakes of Him will never again know spiritual hunger. He said, "I am the light of the world..." (John 8:12). Those who join Jesus as one of His disciples will not be ignorant of spiritual matters but will have the power of understanding, especially of the spiritual truth that brings eternal life. "I am the gate; whoever enters through me will be saved..." (John 10:9). Salvation is only found through Jesus; He is the gate to the Kingdom.

"I am the good shepherd..." (John 10:11). Our Shepherd knowingly and willingly died to save us, because there was no other way. Jesus said to her, "I am the resurrection and the life..." (John 11:25). This is an amazing statement. Jesus has promised even though a believer experiences physical death, he will still have life. Jesus answered, *"I am the way and the truth and the life. No one comes to the Father except through me."* (John 14:6). There is no other way into the presence of God than by accepting the Lord's death as payment in full for our sins. Finally, Jesus said, *"I am the vine; you are the branches. If a man remains in me and I in him, he will bear much fruit; apart from me you can do nothing."* (John 15:5). If we yield our life to Him, (Romans 12:1 – 2) and respond to the prompting of the Holy Spirit He sent to guide us, (John 14:26) we can bear much fruit.

Eddie James recorded a great song simply entitled "I Am". I pray that you will take a listen and allow the words of the song to minister to you and remind you that the great "**I AM**" is watching over you, in all things.
http://www.youtube.com/watch?v=JAX7TXvQZ0U

Father, thank You for being our everything! In You, we live, we move, and we have our being. All that we are and will ever be is in and because of You, and we thank You for that. We pray that we will continue growing in Your grace into the fullness of who You are because You are our great "I Am". In Jesus' name. Amen.

Chapter 8 ~ The Joy of Being a Kept Woman!

**BELIEVING IN THE GOODNESS OF THE LORD
HELPS TO KEEP US IN HIS PERFECT PEACE.**

****

The costs of intimate partner violence in the US alone exceed $5.8 billion per year: $4.1 billion are for direct medical and health care services, while productivity losses account for nearly $1.8 billion.

How many times have you heard someone referred to as being kept by a man? It's called different things, but it all leads to the same conclusion. Depending on your opinion of it, you were either judgmental (she's a tramp) or envious (wishing you had a sugar daddy). Some women love what they consider the sweet life, with a man taking care of their every need. (When done God's way, a married woman with a good husband who provides for her needs is known as a wife.)

I spent too many years **pretending** to be a kept woman. I was married to a man who was both a cheat and abusive. But I pretended to everyone, sometimes, even to myself, that he was a good husband and he loved me. I pretended that he provided the financial and emotional support I needed. I pretended that he kept me happy.

Today, I am proud to say that I **am** truly a kept woman! I don't care what you think of me. If you want to judge me, go ahead. But, if you are envious, I do understand. I have the best keeper any woman (or man) could ever ask for. He knows my every need, even when I fail to ask. He is able to supply me with everything I could ever need or want because He owns it all. If I am sick, He is my healer. If I am lonely, He is my Comforter. When I'm in trouble, He is my Deliverer. If I am down, He is the lifter up of my head. If someone comes against me, He is my Protector. I am a kept woman, I tell you, and I am mighty proud of it. When I think of it all, I am overcome with gratitude and love for my God, knowing that He is my keeper. He is my everything; and without Him, I am nothing.

Maybe you are an independent woman, and you don't need a man to take care of you. I am not. In my own strength, I am weak. But that's alright, because I know I can lean on the everlasting arm of the Lord. In my own mind, I get confused. But that's alright, because my mind has been renewed by the power of the Holy Ghost. I am a kept woman, and I am kept by the only Man who was, who is, and who will ever be. I never have to be concerned about His walking out on me (He promised never to leave me) or failing me in any way (He cannot fail). I am a kept woman, which makes me a blessed woman with a story to tell. I can live in His presence on purpose with a purpose in perfect peace because He is my keeper. *"Oh, to be kept by Jesus, Lord at Thy feet, I fall. Life would be nothing, NOTHING! No, nothing, Thou shall be all, all and all!"* He is my keeper!

Father, thank You for being my keeper! I am so grateful to keep You for keeping me, protecting me, and providing for my every need. Your lovingkindness is so amazing to me – I will always be in awe of Your limitless love. Thank You for all that You are to me. In Jesus' name. Amen.

****

ANYONE CAN GIVE UP, IT'S THE EASIEST THING IN THE WORLD TO DO. BUT TO HOLD IT TOGETHER WHEN EVERYONE ELSE WOULD UNDERSTAND IF YOU FELL APART, THAT'S TRUE STRENGTH.
Anonymous

Chapter 9 ~ Living with Purpose

YOUR PURPOSE IN LIFE IS TO FIND YOUR PURPOSE
AND GIVE YOUR WHOLE HEART AND SOUL TO IT.
(Gautama Buddha)

****

Almost one-third of female homicide victims that are reported in police records are killed by an intimate partner.[7]

How often do you stop and think that life is good? Probably not often enough! But life really is good, particularly if you choose to look at it that way. Shift your focus and you will see that life is good because our God is good. I am not minimizing the real issues of poverty and disease that we face. But, really, most of us are abundantly blessed. Overflowing joy. Blessed peace. Amazing grace. The love of God. We are abundantly blessed. Our failure to recognize our blessings comes from the fact that our focus is on the wrong things.

From the time we are old enough to walk and talk, we are taught that our goal in life is to acquire stuff and things. We compete all the way through school to be the best student, the best athlete, the best debater on the team, the best, the best, we best. We take those drives into college and into our working life. We often-time work overtime, chasing after the American dream. Our house has to be bigger, our car has to be newer, our children have to be brighter, in order for us to feel successful. We are continually seeking more, and more never seems to be enough.

We will never feel satisfied until we realize that what we are really seeking is purpose. It's in all of us, but we need to recognize it and

---

[7] Federal Bureau of Investigation, *Uniform Crime Reports* "Crime in the United States, 2000," (2001).

seek to fulfill it. No matter what that looks like in our lives, it is our reason for being here. And we can never experience the fullness of our good lives without living out our God-given purpose.

Moses stammered, but he was created to be a spokesman for God. Jacob was a liar and a cheat, but he was created to be the progenitor of the nation of Israel. David was an adulterer and a murderer, but he was created to be a man after God's own heart. Paul was a persecutor of the church, but he was created to be one of the greatest proponents of it to have ever lived. Each of these great men of God spent their early years seeking to have meaning in their lives, but they did not begin to fully live until they stepped into the purpose for which they were created.

Even though I *felt* so desperate that I had almost no hope, something within me would not give up. I didn't believe that I had been born just to exist and die. I felt strongly that there was something *specific* for which I had been created. And I felt just as strongly that I would live and not die until I had been given the opportunity to fulfill that purpose. I knew that it would never come to pass in my current living conditions. What I couldn't figure out (at the time) was how to get out and be able to discover what God had in mind for me when He created me.

My journey toward my purpose was painful. But I believe that every step along the way helped to prepare me to be ready to fulfill my destiny. The rejection I felt drove me to seek God all the more. My need to be loved caused me to develop a real desire to know Him through His Word. My physical pain and the shame of my life drew me into a sincere prayer life. It was not the best of times. But it was the time which helped me to know, without a doubt, that without the Lord, I never would have made it!

We may not feel that what we do matters, but it matters to God. His purpose for us, lived out daily as we walk into our destinies, is unique for each of us. And when we are living out our ordained purpose, life is good! Like an intricate puzzle, every piece is needed to complete the picture. We were created on purpose for a purpose. There is nothing more fulfilling in life than living our lives according to God's divine plan.

Father, thank You for creating us with purpose for a purpose. It feels good to know that we are a part of your divine plan. You know that we have an innate need to be needed. Direct our paths and give us ears to hear as You lead us into our destinies. In Jesus' name. Amen.

> **YOU MAY ENCOUNTER MANY DEFEATS, BUT YOU MUST NOT BE DEFEATED. IN FACT, IT MAY BE NECESSARY TO ENCOUNTER THE DEFEATS, SO YOU CAN KNOW WHO YOU ARE, WHAT YOU CAN RISE FROM, HOW YOU CAN STILL COME OUT OF IT.**
> Maya Angelou

Chapter 10 ~ You Are Special to God

LOVE IS A FRUIT IN SEASON AT ALL TIMES AND WITHIN THE REACH OF EVERY HAND.
(Mother Teresa)

****

Around the world, at least one in every three women has been beaten, coerced into sex or otherwise abused during her lifetime. Most often, the abuser is a member of her own family.

It feels good when someone treats you special. You know how it is – someone honors you for some reason – it's your day. You have a birthday and someone celebrates you – it's your day. You are acknowledged for doing something special or important at work – it's your day. You feel appreciated, you feel loved, and it makes you feel special.

We recently celebrated an extraordinary day in my family. It was my father's birthday, the 18th birthday of my late brother's daughter, and the 1st birthday of my late brother's first granddaughter – yeah! Three generations celebrating life on this one day. What a beautiful blessing from the Lord. That was their special day, but to us, they are special every day because we love them.

Coming out of a fifteen-year abusive marriage, I felt anything but special. I was wounded, inside and out. I was bruised, but I was determined not to be bitter. I had survived, and that gave me hope! I had endured, and that was my promise! I was alive, and that gave me purpose! So what if I had to tell myself daily that I was loveable and I was loved? So what if I wasn't hearing it from anyone else? So what if all I had to lean upon was the love that God has for me? I came to know that His love was enough!

Knowing that I was special to God, and loved by Him, was liberating and empowering force which has kept me from that day to this.

Whether or not anyone else tells you so, I want to remind you that you **are also** special – everyday – because God loves you! You don't have to wait for a particular day or time to know that you are exceptional. God has said that you are special in so many ways. And if the God of the universe has said it ... you can believe it ... you are special.

- ➢ You are the apple of His eye (Psalm 17:8)
- ➢ You are fearfully and wonderfully made (there is no one like you) (Psalm 139:14)
- ➢ You are written on the palm of His hand (Isaiah 49:16)
- ➢ You are one of God's children (John 12:36)
- ➢ You are a friend of God (John 15:13)
- ➢ You are righteous (Romans 3:22)
- ➢ You are justified (Romans 5:1)
- ➢ You are accepted in the beloved (Ephesians 1:6)
- ➢ You are holy (I Peter 1:15)

You are special! That ought to give you a new attitude; I know that it did for me. God says that you are somebody. He loves you with a selfless love, a love which is wider and deeper and broader than you can ever imagine. His love is so amazing. Accept it. Live in it. Walk in it. And share it with everyone you meet. After all, they are special too, and they need love just like you.

Father, thank You for making us special, for calling us out of darkness, for making us Your own. Thank You for adopting us into Your royal family, making us a part of Your kingdom, heirs and joint-heirs with Christ. It is amazing to us that You could love us so much, but we thank You that You do. In Jesus' name. Amen.

Chapter 11 ~ Victorious Living

THERE CAME A TIME WHEN THE RISK TO REMAIN TIGHT IN THE BUD WAS
MORE PAINFUL THAN THE RISK IT TOOK TO BLOSSOM.
(Anais Nin)

****

Ninety-two percent of women surveyed listed reducing domestic violence and sexual assault as their top concern.

Jesus lived, died, and rose from the grave in order to redeem us to Himself. That is an amazing kind of love! While in the grave, He took back the keys to hell and death. When He got up, He declared *"all power is in My hands"*. In another place He said, *"I am He who lives, and was dead, and behold, I am alive forevermore. Amen. And I have the keys of Hades and of Death"* (Revelation 1:18). Jesus conquered the grave, and therefore, death has no dominion over those of us who believe.

Only Jesus can save and destroy, can kill and make alive. Death and Hades are still under His dominion. He is the resurrection and the life. On His way from earth to glory, He imputed His power to us. Wow! Another wonderful gift from the Giver of all good and perfect gifts. Abundant life in the earth. Freedom from sin and death. Power over evil. Justified. Sanctified. And waiting to be glorified. Wow!

We have it all. But what are we doing with it? Are we living abundantly? Are we living as people who are freed from sin? Are we exercising our power over evil? Are we living our best lives **now**? Let's be honest. For most of us, the answer is no! So, we need to ask ourselves "why aren't we?". Since God laid out such a beautiful plan, and Jesus gave His life to fulfill the plan, why is so hard for us to live out His plan? The work has been done and the price has been paid. What's holding us back from living with the power and authority that Jesus died for us to have?

I am walking on top of what used to be on top of me! The Lord kept me through every storm of my life. When I made it through to the other side, I was determined to go forward in faith and full confidence in Him. If he could deliver me from fifteen years of abuse – **stronger than ever before**, if He could heal me from stage three breast cancer – **stronger than ever before**, if he could restore the strength of my heart when it was so weak that I should have been confined to a bed – **stronger than ever before**, I can know with a certainty that there is nothing and no one who can stand in my way!

Since you're reading this, you, too, are alive and well, which means you have been given one more opportunity to show God your appreciation for His blessings. That means it is not too late to check your attitude and change your outlook. That means that you have been given one more chance to walk in the fullness of God's gifts to you.

Jesus was the express image of God. Yet, He never once failed to be all that He was while in the earth. He never once failed to glorify God as Father. Paul admonishes us that we should be all that Jesus died for us to be. He warned us against getting caught up in philosophies and ideals according to what someone thinks. Our faith must be in Jesus as Savior **and** Lord of our lives.

Tasha Cobbs sings, "There is power in the name of Jesus to break every chain,..." We have to **know** this, then live our lives accordingly. *"Let your light so shine before men, that they may see your good works and glorify your Father in heaven"* (Matthew 5:16). Victorious living brings glory to the name of our God. Victorious living is faith and worship in action.

Father, thank You for completely equipping and empowering us to live victoriously in the earth. Sadly, it seems that we have more confidence in eternal life than we do in our abundant lives here. Help us to live like Jesus' lived, in the fullness of who we are in You, even as we seek to live to Your glory. In Jesus' name. Amen.

The question isn't who's going to let me; it's who is going to stop me.

Ayn Rand

Chapter 12 ~ Prisoner of Hope

> **WE MUST ACCEPT FINITE DISAPPOINTMENT,**
> **BUT NEVER LOSE INFINITE HOPE.**
> (Martin Luther King, Jr.)

****

Everyday in the US, more than three women are murdered by their husbands or boyfriends.

The Bible is filled with wonderful stories of heroes, men and women of faith and power, whose life stories are recorded so that we might know and trust in the faithfulness of God. We read of Adam and Eve, Abraham and Sarah, Noah, Moses, David, Solomon, Ruth, Esther, Isaiah, Jeremiah, Micah, Hosea, Matthew, Mark, Luke, John, Paul, and Jesus. From Genesis to Revelation, we see the faithfulness of God recorded in the Book of Life as told by these amazing men and women of God.

One thing which is common to most of these is that God's timing was not their timing. God made promises to them, then sent them to live their lives until the timing was right for the fulfillment of those promises. God is a miracle-working God. Most of the time, however, there is a time of working and waiting from the time of His promise to the realization of the promised. All you need to do is read their stories, and you will clearly see that God promised, they waited, God delivered.

They didn't wait idly. Rather, as they waited, they worked and prayed and hoped and believed God. Abraham was 75 when God promised him an heir; he was 100 when he received his son Isaac. David was a young boy (about 13) when God anointed him as the second king over His people; he was a man of 30 when he ascended to the throne of both Judah and Israel. Joseph was a young boy of 17 when he dreamed of greatness; he was a young man almost thirty years old when he became the prime minister of Egypt.

I was a young pre-teen girl when God placed a passion to teach in my heart. I thought that dream would be realized by my teaching in the public schools of Alabama. Not! What He did for me, though, was allow that passion to be used for His glory by equipping me to teach His Word. I don't know if I would have taught school with the same fervor that I have for teaching the Word of God, but I am grateful that He used the desire He placed in me for His glory. The Word of God is like fire in my belly! I want to share it, to use it to build up my sisters and brothers, and it is a constant source of joy in my life.

God is faithful. Once He makes you a promise, it **will** come to pass. Wait for it, trust in it, believe it because it will happen! Don't give up. Keep moving by faith toward your goal, even if you can't see it. Keep your eyes on God; He knows where you are going. Never lose hope! God's timing is not the same as ours, but we should be grateful that it is perfect. God's patience and longsuffering toward us is a blessing. Imagine where we would be if He repaid us for all that we have done against Him! Just as we praise Him for His longsuffering, praise Him for His faithfulness. Your blessing is already in place. God is simply moving us into position to receive it. Never give up. Commit yourself to being a prisoner of hope. Like the heroes of faith, your victory is assured.

Father, thank You that Your Word is true and that we can depend upon it. Help us to remember that You cannot lie, and every promise which You have given us will come to pass. Help us, O Lord, to be prisoners of hope, never giving up, but trusting in You for everything that we need. In Jesus' name. Amen.

Chapter 13 ~ Triumphant in Spite of My Limp

OUT OF SUFFERING HAVE EMERGED THE STRONGEST SOULS;
THE MOST MASSIVE CHARACTERS ARE SEARED WITH SCARS.
(Khalil Gibran)

****

Based on reports from 10 countries, between 55 percent and 95 percent of women who had been physically abused by their partners had never contacted non-governmental organizations, shelters, or the police for help.

Have you ever experienced hurt? Pain? Disappointment? A failed relationship? Disillusionment? Humiliation? Sickness in your body? Financial hardship? Seriously? You are probably wondering, "Who hasn't?" Do you wonder why God allows us to go through so much? We live in a broken world, a world tainted and stained by sin. The result of sin is death, beginning with spiritual death and continuing through physical deaths in many different forms.

Steve Jobs said, *"Your time is limited, so don't waste it living someone else's life. Don't be trapped by dogma – which is living with the results of other people's thinking. Don't let the noise of other's opinions drown out your own inner voice. And most important, have the courage to follow your heart and intuition. They somehow already know what you truly want to become. Everything else is secondary."* Though it came to me in many different ways, that advice is what helped me to live my life triumphantly, in spite of my limp.

Sometimes, God allows us to go through things which are the consequence of our own bull-headedness. We are too stubborn to take instruction or accept direction. We are like the children of Israel, marching around in our own wilderness because in our hard-heartedness, we refuse to obey God. So, the Lord has to allow us to experience some things before we get it right. We tend to go round and round the same mountain over and over again before we finally submit and realize that His will must be done.

At other times, know that God is preparing us for greatness. No one, from the Bible to today, has been able to effectively minister in an area where they have not been broken. If a person is to have an effective witness, it must come from their area of brokenness. The thing which caused the most pain, the most humiliation, cost the most of yourself is the very thing that, once God fixes it, He then says *"Go and tell it!" "Tell it? I can barely stand to think about it. What will they think of me? I don't want to remember that. I would rather never speak of it again."* But God continues saying, *"Go and tell it!"*

I lived for fifteen years in an abusive relationship. It broke me down! I lost myself completely because the who I saw looking back at me from the mirror was not the person that I thought she was. I became all the things I hated – weak, liar, hypocrite, afraid.

Only when I surrendered to God's leading did the real healing begin. As the Lord used my pain to heal that pain in someone else, He provided healing for my own wounds. When I began to take my focus off the thing as it related to me, God restored my soul, He restored my joy, He anointed my testimony, and caused me to live again.

Lashun Pace says it well in her song "For My Good": *"Things I've gone through in life, I thought were too hard for me to bear. The enemy tried some time to make me feel just like God did not care. But I remember reading in God's Word where He said He wouldn't put more on me than I could bear. Yes, Jesus cares and all that I've endured was only for my good. Now I know it was for my good, but for His glory"*.

What is your area of vulnerability? Where are you the weakest? You may have asked the Lord many times why He allowed "it" to happen to you. I challenge you today to not ask that question. Rather, ask how He wants you to use your setback as a testimony in His kingdom. God loves us too much to allow us to suffer without a purpose. Please, don't waste your hurt. Use it to encourage someone else and give God the glory.

*Father, even though we do not want to go through the pain, help us to be thankful to You for everything we go through. The awesome truth is that we go **through**, we endure, and we make it out to the other side by Your grace. We know that Your Word is true, and Your Word has promised us that it all works together for our good. Every hurt, every disappointment, every downturn in our lives is only preparing us for the good things You have prepared for us. We love You so much, and we thank You and give You glory for all that You are to us. In Jesus' name. Amen.*

THE PAST SHOULD BE LEFT IN THE PAST OR IT CAN STEAL YOUR HAPPINESS. LIVE FOR WHAT TOMORROW CAN BRING YOU AND NOT WHAT YESTERDAY HAS TAKEN AWAY. EVERY DAY IS A GIFT.

www.daveswordsofwisdom.com

Chapter 14 ~ Stay in the Fight

REST WHEN YOU'RE WEARY. REFRESH AND RENEW YOURSELF, YOUR BODY, YOUR MIND, YOUR SPIRIT. THEN GET BACK TO WORK.
(Ralph Martson)

****

Men who as children witnessed their parents' domestic violence were twice as likely to abuse their own wives than sons of nonviolent parents.

Satan came with one agenda. He is determined to beat God! His plan to do that is based on his destroying the people who God loves. Jesus said that the devil came to "kill, steal, and destroy". We mean nothing to him; we are only casualties in his war against God. His fight is against the most-high God because he wants to **be** the most-high God. He lost his place in heaven in his effort to take God's place. Can you imagine that?

The result of his continual fight against the saints is that we get tired! That's his goal. *"And he shall speak words against the Most High (God) and shall wear out the saints of the Most High and think to change the time (of sacred feasts and holy days) and the law; and the saints shall be given into his hand for a time, two times, and half a time (three and one-half years)."* (Daniel 7:25 Amplified) We sing songs about it – "It's So Hard to Get Along", "Climbing the Rough Side of the Mountain", "Holding On", and on, and on. We love to lament about how hard our Christian walk is. We wear our struggles like badges of honor. We sound as though we are proud of having issues in our lives. And we act as though we win our battles through our own strength.

When we get tired, it's okay to rest. Take a break. Refresh yourself. Renew your mind. But know when you stop off on the side of the road of life, it is with the intent of getting what you need to be able to continue your journey. That means different things to different people. To me, it's taking vacations each year.

It allows me the time to partake in the things I enjoy. It refreshes me mind, body, and spirit, and it fans the flames of my love for God.

Winners don't quit; giving up is counterintuitive to who we are. We just aren't built that way. Winners win! And we believers are winners, because the Captain of the Host has declared us victorious.

If we believe the scripture, we know that our journey really isn't hard. The difficulties come from our trusting in ourselves rather than God. Don't misunderstand. I'm not minimizing the trials of life. I've had more than my share. Jesus made it clear in John 16:33 that we would have struggles. *"These things I have spoken to you, that in Me you may have peace. In the world you will have tribulation; but be of good cheer, I have overcome the world."* You have to ask yourself: would He tell us to be happy about our situations if He weren't in control of them? In His Word, He promises us rest, comfort, deliverance, peace, joy, hope, security, victory, and abundant life.

Life is filled with swift transitions, and lots of issues do come up in life. But our God has given us His rich promises in His Word that He will be with us through them all. He has provided us with His Spirit to lead and guide us. We have a purpose for being here, and we owe it to the Lord to fulfill our purpose. We cannot allow the issues of life to cause us to quit. We have to stay in the fight! There is someone along our paths who needs what we have to offer, so we cannot stop. There is too much work to do.

Don't ever forget that the devil is a liar, and the father of lies. But God is not a man that He should lie. You decide – whose report will you believe? Yur outlook on life, and how we handle the challenges of life, is fully dependent on your answer. We may get tired, but we have to stay in the fight. We cannot give up. There is too much depending on us.

Father, thank You for the assurance of knowing that we are victorious in You. You have promised us that we can always lean and depend upon You. Give us the wisdom to choose to do just that. We need You, and we cannot make it through this life without You. Yet, we make choices every day without asking for Your guidance. Forgive us for our arrogance and self-confidence which draws us away from You. Help us to humbly submit our wills to Yours. In Jesus' name, Amen.

LIFE GOES BY SO FAST, OUR TIME IS SHORT. NO REPLAYS, NO REWINDS. SO ENJOY EACH AND EVERY MOMENT AS IT COMES.

www.daveswordsofwisdom.com

GOD IS A GOD OF RESTORATION. WHEN WE PLACE THE BROKEN PIECES OF OUR LIVES IN HIS HANDS, HE RESTORES THEM TO A BEAUTY THAT FAR OUTSHINES THE FORMER.

Chapter 15 ~ The Journey is the Destination

I DON'T WANT TO GET TO THE END OF MY LIFE AND FIND THAT I LIVED JUST THE LENGTH OF IT. I WANT TO HAVE LIVED THE WIDTH OF IT AS WELL.
(Diane Ackerman)

****

Fifty-six percent of women who experience any partner violence are diagnosed with a psychiatric disorder. Twenty-nine percent of all women who attempt suicide were battered, 37% of battered women have symptoms of depression, 46% have symptoms of anxiety disorder, and 45% experience post-traumatic stress disorder.[8]

I heard Donald Lawrence say during a concert that oftentimes when he is listening to a Biblical teaching, he can "hear" the cadence and rhythm of what is being taught as lyrics to a song. That is his gift, his calling in life, and he is good at it. He has written hit songs which he and his groups have recorded, and he has written many hit songs for other artists. He learned his purpose a long time ago and has been walking in the favor of God since he started fulfilling that purpose.

I feel the same way about writing. I see something, hear something, smell something, touch something – it doesn't matter – as I experience life, I often "see" a spiritual implication which excite me. It's the way God speaks to me and leads me through many of my life situations. So when I saw this book entitled, *"The Journey is the Destination"*, it was another "aha" moment for me.

---

[8] Kirstie K. Danielson et al., *Comorbidity Between Abuse of an Adult and DSM-III-R Mental Disorders: Evidence From an Epidemiological Study*, 155 Am. J. of Psychiatry 131 (1998)

The book tells the story of Dan Eldon, a young artist who was killed just as he began life as an adult. The following quote is taken from an overview that I read about the book: *"Reinvention is a journey that starts right where you are. It's about assessing what is working for you and what is not. Lean into the idea of small steps leading to big results. Learn the process to get clarity, the steps to rediscovering your purpose, and what motivates you both personally and professionally."*

When I was in the midst of the most violent period of my marriage, I sunk into a dark hole. I was so tired, and barely functioning. I was the sole breadwinner and just barely making minimum wage. But God! We got by with the help of the Lord. He kept opening doors during that time which even now just blow my mind. But in spite of that, I was in a dark place. I was sad all the time. When I wasn't working, all I wanted to do was sleep. But I couldn't get a good night's rest because my mind would not shut down. I was alone, because my husband was spending his nights with one of his many women. He came home to eat, shower, and take out his frustrations on me, but he spent his "good" times with others.

So, I struggled to keep it all together, to be mother, wife to a part-time husband, and a perfect saint on Sunday mornings. I sang in the choir, taught Sunday school, and led the women and youth groups. But I was dead inside, and no one seemed to notice. Thank God that He sent Jesus as the "resurrection and the life"!

Most of spend too much of our lives trying to be what we "think" others want us to be. We have so many faces that we forget what we look like! But God created each of us with our own unique purpose. Each of us has that one thing (or two) which drives us, which excites us, which brings us joy, and gives us a sense of purpose. When we discover our place of purpose, we can begin walking with confidence into our destinies. It is in this place that we will find the fullness of the good life in God. It is in this place that we will find the rest of God which will bring peace to our souls. It is in this place that we will know that the journey **is** the destination.

Have you ever taken a great road trip? You know, the kind of trip you keep talking about until your friends and family get tired of hearing about. Norton Juster said, "*The most important reason for going from one place to another is to see what's in between,....*" The best road trip is one with no real agenda except to enjoy the journey. You don't have to be anywhere according to a schedule. Instead, you stop and sightsee along the way, spending the night in different towns along your route. When you get to your final destination, you enjoy it, but it feels like just one more stop along the way, because you enjoyed the journey.

That's the way our lives should be. Not careless or ineffective, but every stop through life should be one which is memorable. We should be excited to tell our stories, and tell them in a way which is fresh every time because we are enjoying our lifes' journeys. We may have some bumps along the way, and even a detour now and then, but we can enjoy the journey as long as we trust God as our guide. Remember, we are taking this journey "in the *rest* of God" (His peace, joy, faith, hope, and love), fulfilling our own unique purpose. We don't have to wait to get to heaven to receive our blessings; if we enjoy the journey, we will live abundantly now. So, what was just labor will become a labor of love. We **know** that our journey **is** our destination when we are living the blessed life!

Father, thank You for ordering our steps and directing our paths on our journey into destiny. Some of us are tired because we have tried to do this on our own. We surrender to You; we want to do it Your way. Help us to rest in You, to trust You, and to follow You on the journey of a lifetime! Do what You need to do in us to make it so. In Jesus' name. Amen.

Chapter 16 ~ A Living Hope

> EVERYONE HAS INSIDE OF HER A PIECE OF GOOD NEWS.
> THE GOOD NEWS IS THAT YOU DON'T KNOW HOW GREAT YOU
> CAN BE! HOW MUCH YOU CAN LOVE! WHAT YOU CAN
> ACCOMPLISH! AND WHAT YOUR POTENTIAL IS!
> (Anne Frank)

****

Reports indicate some 86% of the women who received a protection order state the abuse either stopped or was greatly reduced.[9]

Hope is the confident expectation that what we are looking for will come to pass. I remember a recent lesson study which was subject was "A Living Hope". Taken from the first chapter of I Peter, this lesson was focused on the Son of God as our living hope.

It is in Him that we live, we move, and we have our being. Before Jesus, everyone who died in the Lord died in hope, looking toward the cross and the coming Messiah. But since Jesus has lived, died, and risen from the dead, we have the confidence of knowing that our hope is alive in Him. We have the assurance of eternal life.

Hope is what gave me the strength to place one foot before the other one when all I wanted to do was die. Hope is what kept me seeking God for deliverance. Hope is what I held on to expecting the greater in spite of what I could see with my eyes. Hope is what kept me alive and has given me the renewed determination to live out the rest of my days abundantly. There was quite the wait from my asking to my receiving, but it was worth the wait! God has outdone Himself on my behalf – one more time – and I

---

[9] James Ptacek, *Battered Women in the Courtroom: The Power of Judicial Response* (1999)

wouldn't trade my life for anything except my eternal life with Him.

> **GOD DIDN'T GIVE YOU THE STRENGTH TO GET BACK ON YOUR FEET SO THAT YOU CAN RUN BACK TO THE SAME THING THAT KNOCKED YOU DOWN.**

When God called Abraham out from the land of Ur, He promised him that He was going to bless him. He even said that through Abraham, all the nations of the earth would be blessed. He reiterated this promise in Abraham's son, Isaac, and again to Abraham's grandson, Jacob. God then changed Jacob's name to Israel and established Jacob's children as the twelve tribes through whom He would manifest the promised blessings.

Even though God had spoken to Abraham and gave Him the promise of blessings in his life, Abraham and his descendants did not have what we have today. They had the law, but no direct access to God. Jesus tore down the veil which kept the people out of the holy of holies, thereby giving us direct access to God. Have you thought about how cool that is? Before Christ, the only access to God was through the priests and only at certain times of the year. The priests wore special garments with bells in the hems so that the people would know to remove them from the holy place if God struck them because of their sin. But because of Jesus and the work He did on Calvary, we can go boldly before the throne of grace with the confident hope that God will answer our prayers.

There was a lot of history between God's covenant with Abraham and His sending Jesus to be born in the earth. But praise the Lord – He is faithful! He made a promise to Abraham and his seed, and our God is no shorter than His Word. Because He can neither lie nor change, God was bound to keep His promise. He sent His Son to redeem us unto Himself, and in the process, He provided us with a living hope. In Jesus, we are abundantly blessed.

In Jesus, we have the fulfillment of all that God promised to Abraham all those years ago. Redeemer. Savior. Friend. Brother. Comforter. Counselor. Restorer of the breach. In Jesus, we have a living hope.

Father, thank You for placing an undying hope within our spirits. We have no better focus for our hope than You, because in You, we can confidently look to receive the thing for which we hope. Thank You for Your faithfulness and the assurance of knowing that our hope is secure in You. Thank You for giving us Jesus, our living hope. In Jesus' name. Amen.

GOD IS ABLE TO BRING HOPE INTO YOUR LIFE EVEN WHEN EVERYTHING SEEMS HOPELESS.

(see Jeremiah 29:11)
TRUST IN THE LORD!

Chapter 17 ~ Breaking Free of Fear

"WHAT IS TO GIVE LIGHT MUST ENDURE THE BURNING."
(Eleanor Roosevelt)

****

Females who are 20-24 years of age are at the greatest risk of nonfatal intimate partner violence.

We all know about faith and its importance in our lives. We recognize that "*... without faith, it is impossible to please God*" (Hebrews 11:6). We mistakenly think that doubt is the opposite of faith, but the real antithesis of faith is fear. Fear that God won't come through. Fear that God won't answer our prayers. Fear because we don't know what God requires of us in order to answer our prayers. But, why do we fear? Pastor said it is due to a lack of faith (duh!). But the "aha" is that our lack of faith is not because of doubt, but a lack of knowledge! If we really know God the way we think we know God, we would always respond in faith, no matter what the situation looks like.

I know I may sound like Pollyanna because my life has been interesting! But in spite of the many challenges, I am determined to live it to the fullest. Many of the life challenges I have encountered have caused me to stop, but only for awhile. Some of my stops along the journey were longer than others. At the end of it, I realized they were simply pit stops to allow me to refuel in preparation for completing the trip.

In a crisis situation, what is in us will come out of us. (Can I get an 'amen'?) We are all creatures of habit and if you make good habits, good habits will make you. This wisdom has been around since ancient times. Aristotle once said, "*We are what we repeatedly do. Excellence, then, is not an act but a habit.*" Solomon wrote in Proverbs 23:7, "*For as he thinks in his heart, so is he...*". Our professions of faith are just that until they are tested by the fires of life. It is only then that we know if we really trust God. Then we know if we have complete faith in Him. But until we are faced with that situation, we don't know – not absolutely – how we will respond. That is why it is so important – it is absolutely vital – to immerse ourselves in the Word of God and get to **know** Him.

We go through life on autopilot. The subconscious mind – the habitual mind – is over one million times more powerful than the conscious mind. Most of what we do is handled by our subconscious, no matter how smart we may think we are. Heart beating. Breathing. Blinking. Blood flow. Immune system. Digestive system. We don't have to think about these things; our brains know what to do and they automatically handle them. The subconscious mind is so vast and so powerful that we do not even know what it is thinking or capable of. It truly runs our lives – whether we know it or not! When our automatic systems are affected by disease or abuse, we know the difference. We have to use outside resources to help them do what they once did automatically.

So, what makes us think that we can handle life without having the spiritual resources we need in us? We **need** the Word! We **need** the Holy Spirit "quickened" and not "quenched" by our willful disobedience of Him! We **need** our faith in God, fine-tuned by experience and ready to respond in the heat of battle.

Life comes at us fast, and when it does, we don't have time to **get** ready. We have to **be** ready! Habits begin and manifest deep in the mind. Good habits can make our lives easier, helping us to do the ordinary things of life without thinking about them. If we walk by faith and not by sight daily, every day of our lives, even when things are going well, we can be more confident that we will respond in faith when a crisis arises.

To break self-defeating attitudes and fear-based behaviors, we have to know that we have the power to choose and the power to change. We have the power to let go of old thinking and adopt the mindset of champions of faith. In the words of Joyce Meyer, we have to *"do it afraid"*. When we take that step of faith, it's amazing what God will do. Don't believe me? Try Him! It's up to you.

Father, thank You for giving us a foundation of faith in You. You take us through the right experiences to learn to trust You even more, growing our faith. Even when situations cause us to fear, help us to remember what You did last time and trust Your earnest guarantee of what You will do this time. Help us to build up our faith muscles and believe the promises of Your Word automatically because we know that You are faithful. In Jesus' name. Amen.

> **IF YOU LOOK AT THE WORLD, YOU'LL BE DISTRESSED.
> IF YOU LOOK WITHIN, YOU'LL BE DEPRESSED.
> IF YOU LOOK AT GOD, YOU'LL BE AT REST.**
> Corrie Ten Boom

Chapter 18 ~ The Miracle in You

WHEN WE DO THE BEST WE CAN, WE NEVER KNOW WHAT MIRACLE IS WROUGHT IN OUR LIFE, OR IN THE LIFE OF ANOTHER.
(Helen Keller)

****

Women who experience physcial abuse as children are at a greater risk of victimization as adults, and men have a far greater (more than double) likelihood of perpetrating abuse.[10]

Miracles are manifested in so many different ways. The conception and healthy birth of a child. The transformation of the earth when winter gives ways to spring. A diagnosis of cancer which is suddenly cured. A recovery from a major injury. Blinded eyes are opened. The lame walk again. Each is a miracle which happens every day. Yet, for many of us, we never stop to think that God is working miracles every day of our lives.

We have relegated the miraculous to the Bible days. God parting the Red Sea. God raining down manna to feed His people as they wandered in the wilderness. God causing the sun to stand still to allow Joshua to win the battle. Miracles. Big events. Supernatural happenings that nobody can deny. But what about when He woke you up this morning? Can you deny the miraculous when that car just barely missed you when that driver ran the red light? What happened when your loved one was raised from their sick bed? How did you, the least qualified applicant, secure that wonderful job? Our God from the Bible is still working miracles; we just need to have our eyes opened so that we can see.

---

[10] Family Violence Prevention Fund, *The Facts on Children and Domestic Violence*

The thirty-seventh chapter of Ezekiel records one of God's "big miracles". In this account, Ezekiel has a vision regarding dry bones in a valley. This passage has been preached so many times, and always so dramatically, that most of us know the account by heart. It speaks to God's omnipotence. It is evidence of God's omniscience. But the essence of the vision is God's loving care for His people, Israel, and His assurance to them that He would ever leave them or forsake them. God promised that He would bring them out of their captivity and restore them to their former glory.

He makes a point of telling us that this valley was full of bones, and the bones were very dry. They had been in this state for a long time. In the natural, there was no life or essence of any kind left within them. They were **very** dry. If these bones were going to live again, it would come only through the miraculous hand of an all-knowing and all-powerful God. Such was Ezekiel's response when rhetorically asked if the bones could live. Ezekiel replied, "Lord, You know".

God was the only one who could cause the bones to live again. At His command, skin and flesh covered them. The wind was told to blow upon them, restoring them to life. The wind represented the Spirit of God, and clearly showed His quickening powers. The vision was to encourage the Jews, to remind them of both their restoration after the captivity, and also their recovery from their present and long-continued dispersion. This vision was also a clear intimation of the resurrection of the dead. It shows us that even the most hopeless sinner can be saved under the power and grace of God.

Still looking for a miracle? Take a look at yourself, once total lost in sin. Dead in trespasses and sin. Dead. Dry. **Very** dry in your spirit which was separated from God. But when you said yes!, God's Spirit quickened your spirit and brought new life. Thank God every day that You responded to His voice when He asked you, "Can you live again?" Thank Him for the quickening power of His Holy Spirit. Thank Him for new life in Christ.

Father, thank You for giving us new life in You. We praise You that in You we live, we move, and we have our being. You are the very air we breathe! We know that we were once dead in our trespasses and sins. We are so grateful that we have been born again into Your glorious Kingdom, never to die again. In Jesus' name. Amen.

EVERY STRUGGLE IN YOUR LIFE HAS SHAPED YOU INTO THE PERSON YOU ARE TODAY. BE THANKFUL FOR THE HARD TIMES; THEY HAVE MADE YOU STRONGER.

Chapter 19 ~ I'm Brand New!

I DON'T WANT TO THINK OF ALL THE MISERY BUT OF THE BEAUTY THAT STILL REMAINS.
(Ann Franks)

****

African-American women face higher rates of domestic violence than white women, and American-Indian women are victimized at a rate more than double that of women of other races.[11]

We have been given a "do-over"! Isn't that just the coolest thing? Born in sin, we received salvation by the grace of God through faith. By faith, we have been given new life, and we don't ever have to look back at what was.

Israel Houghton expresses it well in his song, "Moving Forward". He sings, "I'm not going back, I'm moving ahead. Here to declare to You my past is over. In You, all things are made new, surrendered my life to Christ. I'm moving, moving forward."[1]

That should be all of our testimonies. Jesus died so that we could move forward and not look back. We are free from the penalty and the power of sin. We have been made holy and righteous. We have been sanctified and are waiting to be glorified. There is nothing in our past worth returning to. Our future is ahead of us.

Why, then, do you think we so easily slip back into our old ways? Everything about our new life in Christ is good. All the Lord asks in return is that we live so that He is honored and His name is glorified. That means changing the way we think. We have to renew our minds. That mean changing the way we talk. We cannot bless God and curse others out of the same mouth. That

---

[11] Bureau of Justice Statistics, *Victim Characteristics: Race*

means not giving in to Satan's temptations. We must focus on the things of God.

God gave us a "do-over"! There aren't many things that offer us second chances. But God has given us new life in Him, and it's better than anything we thought we had the first time. It honors Him when we keep moving forward.

Father, thank You for making us new in You. You have equipped us with all we need to mature into a likeness of You. Give our hearts the desire to emulate You in all areas of our lives, renewing our minds daily through Your Word. In Jesus' name. Amen.

> **YOU HAVE TO ACCEPT WHATEVER COMES AND THE ONLY IMPORTANT THING IS THAT YOU MEET IT WITH COURAGE AND WITH THE BEST THAT YOU HAVE TO GIVE.**
> Eleanor Roosevelt

****

THE FIVE P'S OF A STRONG WOMAN
A STRONG WOMAN KNOWS
* **WHEN TO PUSH**
* **WHEN TO PULL**
* **WHEN TO PLAN**
* **WHEN TO BE PATIENT**
* **WHEN TO PRAY**
www.YouBetterPreach.com

Chapter 20 ~ My Battle Scars of Victory

>NEVER BE ASHAMED OF THE SCARS THAT LIFE HAS LEFT YOU WITH.
>A SCAR MEANS THAT HURT IS OVER, THE WOUND IS CLOSED,
>YOU ENDURED THE PAIN, AND GOD HAS HEALED YOU."
>(Facebook 2013)

****

Domestic violence thrives when we are silent; but if we take a stand and work together, we can end domestic violence.

If you have ever had an injury, you know that the first step in the healing process is the scab. When the skin is injured, a healthy body immediately begins repairing itself. Most people take scabs and the healing process for granted without ever considering how the body can do this with little or no outside intervention. Understanding scab formation and skin healing is important; any disruption will prolong the healing process.

Immediately the body closes off broken blood vessels to slow the bleeding. It then fills the injury site with fluid that contains platelets, fibrin and other blood cells so that no more blood and lymph substances can be lost. The hole-filling fluid forms a plug that dries and creates a protective layer over the injury site. This protective layer is usually referred to as a scab. The scab keeps bacteria and other substances out, preventing irritation and infection.

While the scab is shielding the injury from the intrusion of bacteria and other substances, work is going on underneath to restore the surface of the skin. The body repairs the damage by filling in the hole left by the injury with new cells. When this process is complete, the scab will fall off to reveal normal, healthy skin underneath.

Peeling off the scab too soon can cause further irritation or infection. This is why it is important not to pull at a scab or remove it; rather, let it fall off on its own. Removing a scab before it is ready will certainly prolong the healing time, and could lead to unnecessary scarring.

I need to let you know that there is a second definition for scab. It is a contemptible person. And that can also be a part of the healing process. I thank God I have completely forgiven him, but my ex-husband was a contemptible person. He was mean and hateful, and he tried to destroy my very soul by breaking down my mind, my will, and my emotions. But **ONE DAY, MY SOUL OPENED UP!!!** I didn't know it, but God's angels had immediately gone to work on restoring my soul each time he came against it. They would close off the bleeding by drawing me into prayer and meditation. The Holy Spirit would speak comfort to me, placing a protective layer over the injured site. As He covered me, work on going on underneath to restore my soul. Unbeknown to me, my spirit was getting stronger, and I was becoming.

I peeled off my covering a few times, and I had some setbacks. My healing took longer as a result. But though it was delayed, it was not denied! I have some physical scars, but my soul is healed! My spirit-woman is strong and still growing stronger.

A scar is caused by the body producing a protein of collagen fibers to knit the skin together and repair the wound; this is triggered by a gap in the skin or inflammation. To minimize scarring, you must minimize the extent of the injury.

The closer together the sides of the cut are, the less chance there is of scarring – or at least the thinner the scar will be. Cover the wound loosely with a bandage or breathable dressing. Covering the cut completely will stop air getting to it, and so delay the healing process; too much air causes hard scabs to form, which can increase the risk of scarring. Always keep the wound clean:

any infection is sure to delay healing, which can also lead to scarring.

Scar tissue looks and feels different from regular body tissue. Usually, scars are flat and lightly colored. Sometimes, however, the body will be off in production of collagen, producing too much or too little. When this happens, the scars that form may look and feel different. When the body produces too much collagen, raised scars called keloids are formed.

I have some scars, from beatings, from surgery, and even some accidents which had nothing to do with either. But in spite of my scars, I am healed – physically, emotionally, and spiritually. My scar tissue looks a little different, but that is in appearance only. I have scars, but I am healed. I walked away from some of the toughest battles in my life with all of me intact. No headaches, and no more heartache. No sleepless nights. No fears. No dread. Each day dawns with wondrous anticipation and expectation.

The scars that we have are our battle scars, and they are our proof that we won! It doesn't matter if they are noticeable to everyone or only visible to us, like my surgery scar. It doesn't matter if they are raised keloids or sunken areas on your face. Our scars are our evidence of our victory. Who we are is defined by God, and God says we are the best! He loves us. Whatever else that may be going on with you, get over it! God loves you and it is that love which will lead you to your place in Him.

The love of God is what set me free! His love is what stopped me from picking at the scabs which were the mess of my life, allowing them to heal. God loves me – wow!

- ✓ I no longer see myself as a victim – I am victorious!
- ✓ I am not a casualty – I am a conqueror!
- ✓ I am no longer hurting – I have been healed!
- ✓ I no longer suffer in silence – I am a survivor!

- ✓ And thank God I am no longer pitiful – I am powerful!

It is God's amazing love which drew me out of the darkness under which I was hiding, allowing me to breathe again and experience His cleansing. I was desperately looking for love, and it was inside of me all the time. The God who saved me, the God who had kept me, the God who healed me, the God who raised me up, the God who gave me my identity, the God who provided for me, LOVED me! Coming to an understanding of the height and depth and width and breadth of God's love for me brought me to a place of knowing that I could do all things through Him because nothing could separate me from that love.

If you are healing – from abuse, abandonment, neglect, loneliness, fear, regret, unhappiness, depression, addiction, rejection, sickness or disease – don't trip! **YOU ARE HEALING!** Be grateful for your scabs; they are the proof that you are healing. Don't be like me, and pick them off before the healing is complete. It may not look pretty, but it is important in order for you to come through whole again. And praise God every chance you get for your scars, because they are your proof that you survived!

If you want all that God has for you, start believing all that God says about you. My scabs are gone, but I look at my scars now and then to remind myself of how far God has brought me. A scar means that it's time to allow your beauty to rise out of your ashes. Your scars say that it is time for you to live! There is no shame, no regret, and no fear of going back that way again.

****

THE MORE DIFFICULTIES ONE HAS TO ENCOUNTER, WITHIN AND WITHOUT, THE MORE SIGNIFICANT AND THE HIGHER IN INSPIRATION HER LIFE WILL BE.
Horace Bushnell

Chapter 21 ~ Never Give Up!

IT DOESN'T MATTER WHO YOU ARE, OR WHERE YOU CAME FROM.
THE ABILITY TO TRIUMPH BEGINS WITH YOU. ALWAYS.
(Oprah Winfrey)

****

The stigma of being a domestic violence victim continues to be a major issue. It forces victims to miss work, hide, or lie to family and friends at work.

Sometimes, it seems that the world has lost hope. The murder rate in America is staggering – homicides, matricide, patricide, suicide. People are depressed. Oppressed. The divorce rate is at an all time high. Abuse and molestation are rampant. All these sad states of the human condition stem from living life without real hope, without the will to push through, without the determination to win. But we can't give up on God because He won't give up on us.

I remember the period in my life when I felt like I could not take one more step. I was so depressed that I didn't know what joy felt like. Every day was a struggle just to keep it moving. I was sad. I was hopeless. And I was so afraid. But in spite of that, there was something deep down inside of me which would not stop hoping that someday, soon, my life could be better. Deep in the well of my spirit was the indomitable hope that my life **would** be better, my days **would** be brighter, and my destiny **would** be fulfilled.

There is a scene in the movie "The Siege" where the CIA operative says to the FBI agent, "*In this game, the most committed wins.*" She was talking about terrorists, trying to encourage the FBI to diligently pursue their targets because the terrorists would not stop on their mission until they were done or dead! What would happen if we approached life this way?

Where would we find ourselves on the road of life if we, like Jacob, declared, "…"**I will not let You go unless You bless me!**" (Genesis 32:26). We sing that "God's got a blessing for you … You can have it, reach up and grab it!" But, really, do we believe it? If your answer is yes, then ask yourself if there is anything for which you are willing to fight? Is there anything which will cause you to chase after God until you can clearly see where He was leading? Can you find any cause for which you are willing to fight until the death?

Don't get it twisted. I'm not referring to the silly things of life that we so easily get caught up in. I am talking about living life with the joy of the Lord. I am talking about abundant life in God. Victory is often just around the next fork in the road, but we have to keep our eye on the prize, which is Jesus Christ. We shouldn't want our legacy to be that we **almost** succeeded.

Never give up the fight! Persevere. Endure. Hang in there. But don't give up. Remember, the most committed wins.

Father, thank You for the assurance of victory in You. Now, increase our faith so that we believe it! Help us to stand when the storms of life come against. Give us the determination to press into You when we are weakened by the fight. Remind us daily to put on the armor with which You have equipped us so that we are prepared for the attacks of the enemy. We can make it, but only if our hope is in You. In Jesus' name. Amen.

> YOU GAIN STRENGTH, COURAGE, AND CONFIDENCE BY EVERY EXPERIENCE IN WHICH YOU REALLY STOP TO LOOK IN THE FACE OF FEAR. YOU MUST DO THE THING WHICH YOU THINK YOU CANNOT DO.
> Eleanor Roosevelt

Chapter 22 ~ Renew Your Mind

YOU MUST WEED YOUR MIND AS YOU WEED YOUR GARDEN.
(Astrid Alauda)

****

Intimate partner violence results in more than 18.5 million mental health care visits each year.[12]

People seemingly start from the same place, yet they end up in very different ones. Do you ever wonder why some people wither in certain circumstances while others thrive under the same conditions? Why is it that two people can have the same parents, grow up in the same house, and take divergently different paths in life? What makes the difference?

It begins and ends with attitude. A person's outlook on a situation can make all the difference in how they handle it. One woman is abused and lives a live filled with depression and fear. Another one has the same experiences and chooses to reinvent herself, using those experiences to help other women. One person is diagnosed with a terminal disease and withdraws to await death. Another receives the same diagnosis, decides to "live while they are living", and finds a renewed sense of peace and purpose. One person experiences the loss of a loved one and surrenders their life to grief. Another person chooses to celebrate the life of their loved one and appreciate the life they have.

It took me fifteen years to extricate myself from my abuser. Fifteen years! What was I doing during those long,pitiful years? I didn't know it then, but looking back, I realize that I was

---

[12] *Costs of Intimate Partner Violence Against Women in the United States.* 2003. Centers for Disease Control and Prevention, National Centers for Injury Prevention and Control. Atlanta, GA. Tjaden, Patricia & Thoennes, Nancy.

renewing my mind. Through prayer. Through study of the Word. Through surrender to God. Day by day, I was becoming a new creation in Him, and I didn't know it until the day came when He said "**go**!" I realized that within me I had the strength to do things that I never thought possible because I had come to the end of myself. I had surrendered my life into His hands. Through the power of the Holy Spirit, I had renewed my mind!

I know that my mind's renewal was complete because when I walked (**RAN!**) away, I was totally free. No hatred. No bitterness. No unforgiveness. No thoughts of vengeance. Nothing but gratitude to the Lord that He had kept me **and** delivered me. I was free!

A person's attitude is the thing which separates those who are just surviving from those who are thriving and living the abundant life. So, then, the question becomes, how do we develop the winning attitude? How do we go from living under the curse of the enemy to walking in the blessings of the Lord?

Can I say it again? You have to renew your mind! This does not come from wishful thinking. You cannot just think yourself happy. You have to set your mind and meditate on the right things. But the only way to fully and completely renew your mind is by studying the Word of God. It is only in the Word that we find all the answers to living life in the earth and life for all eternity.

The Word provides us with all that we need, but we have to believe it. We have to believe that we have the fruit of Spirit, which affirms that we have love, joy, peace, longsuffering, kindness, goodness, faithfulness, gentleness, and self-control. There is so much power in knowing that you are loved. Knowing that you are loved by the sovereign Jehovah, the God of the universe, is on a whole different level! (Why do you think Satan works so hard to keep you from really accepting God's love?)

If you BELIEVE in your hearts that God loves you, then it will become a lot easier to clear your minds and think on good things. His love will be the key to your renewing your mind.

Father, thank You for giving us new minds in You. Because of Your Spirit and His imparted gifts to us, we know that we are new creatures in You. So, we boldly declare that we will daily renew our minds through Your Word. We invite Your Holy Spirit to refresh us so that we can continue to grow in our knowledge of who You are and all that You are to us. In Jesus' name. Amen.

GREAT SPIRITS HAVE ALWAYS ENCOUNTERED VIOLENT OPPOSITION FROM MEDIOCRE MINDS.
Albert Einstein

~ RESPECT AND TRUST ~
THE TWO EASIEST THINGS IN LIFE FOR SOMEONE TO LOSE AND THE HARDEST THINGS TO GET BACK.

Chapter 23 ~ Now Live – Victoriously!

OUR DEEPEST WISHES ARE WHISPERS OF OUR AUTHENTIC SELVES. WE MUST LEARN TO RESPECT THEM. WE MUST LEARN TO LISTEN.
(Sarah Ban Breathnach)

****

Eight-five percent of domestic violence victims are women!

I once heard T. D. Jakes say "the enemy is 'in-a-me'". Many times, we are our own worst enemy. At times, we put ourselves down based on how other people treat us. Other times, we allow other people to put us down. There are times when we think too highly of ourselves. There are still other times when we don't think highly enough of ourselves. We are complex creatures, seemingly never satisfied. We want "it", got to have "it", then once we get "it", we find that the "thrill is gone". Add to this the continual bombardment of our minds by the devil and his entourage and it doesn't take long to understand what Bishop Jakes means. It's the Joyce Meyer's syndrome of "I want, I think, I feel".

How do you change this exploding battlefield of our minds into victory ground? It's important to us because that is where the war is going on, every day. Satan could care less about your stuff and things; he wants your mind. He only messes with your self-worth, your relationships, your possessions, YOU, so that he can mess with your mind. So, how do you gain control of "your righteous mind"? You can begin by thinking like Jesus thought. There was a popular expression a few years ago, "WWJD – what would Jesus do?" It was very cliché, but it really was on point. If we want to live victoriously, pleasing God with our lives and living in peace with ourselves, we have to allow our minds to become like Jesus'.

Jesus made it clear where He got His instructions. He said, on more than one occasion, that He could do nothing of Himself. He did what He saw the Father doing, He obeyed what the Father told Him, and He said what the Father said. It wasn't because He did not have power of His own, but He recognized that He had been sent to the earth for a purpose. He knew that if He was going to fulfill that purpose, and leave us with irrefutable instructions on how we should live, it had to be aligned with the will of the Father.

One of my favorite "Barbara-isms" is that *"you have to live while you're living!"* We have the power to do that, but we have to take that authority and do it. As the apostle Paul concludes his letter of exhortation and instruction to the Ephesian church, he reminded them of all that God had done to equip them in their war against Satan. *"...as His divine power has given to us all things that pertain to life and godliness, through the knowledge of Him who called us by glory and virtue,..."* (II Peter 1:3). Through the indwelling Holy Spirit, we are equipped for battle. And we are assured of victory.

But the armor is effective only if we use it. Paul admonishes us to be strong in the Lord. We have no strength of our own; it comes from the power of His might. That's alright, because He is well able to support us in His strength. We have to put it on in order to be able to stand. Failure to do so leaves us defenseless and vulnerable. But clothed in the armor of God, we are more than conquerors!

That's all we have to do. There is no magic formula. You don't need to pay tribute or repeat a litany each day. You just have to do what Jesus did. Put on the whole armor of God, then align yourself with the Captain of the hosts. Seek His will (*found in His Word*), trust His direction (*through the Holy Spirit*), and follow Him daily. Put aside your own personal agenda and commit to following God's agenda. He wants **all** of us in total surrender.

The apostle Paul said that God has revealed the mystery of His will to us (Ephesians 3:3 – 5). We no longer have to go to an intermediary for revelation. His will has been revealed to us, but we have to read the Book.

"Now that's how you do it!" (In my Will Smith/Mike Lowery from *Bad Boys* voice....) That's how you take control of YOUR righteous mind and live each day victoriously!

Father, thank You for the revelations found within Your Word. You have made known to us the mystery of Your will, and that is that no man would perish, but all would have everlasting life. Thank You, God, for "so loving us" that You have placed Your Holy Spirit within us. Now, it is up to us to choose to live according to Your will. Give us the strength to live with renewed minds and sincere hearts, seeking to please You with our lives by living each day victoriously. In Jesus' name. Amen.

IF YOU DON'T LIKE BEING A DOORMAT, THEN GET OFF THE FLOOR.
Al Anon

> WHEN WE SPEAK WE ARE AFRAID OUR WORDS
> WILL NOT BE HEARD OR WELCOMED.
> BUT WHEN WE ARE SILENT, WE ARE STILL AFRAID.
> SO IT IS BETTER TO SPEAK.
> Audre Lorde

Chapter 24 ~ The Power of One Voice

THINK TWICE BEFORE YOU SPEAK, BECAUSE YOUR WORDS AND INFLUENCE WILL PLANT THE SEED OF EITHER SUCCESS OR FAILURE IN THE MIND OF ANOTHER.
(Napolean Hill)

****

Approximately 33 million U.S. adults admit they have been a victim of domestic violence.

Martin Luther King, Jr. Betty Friedan. Malcolm X. Oprah Winfrey. Patrick Henry. Helen Gurley Brown. Frederick Douglass. Sylvia Plath. Martin Luther. Eleanor Roosevelt. One person. One voice. And the voice of each one, spoken at the right time, had the power to change the course of history.

Do you know the power of your own voice? I didn't for a very long time. I didn't realize how much I had allowed the negativity of "his" voice drown out the power of "His" voice! *"Life and death are in the power of the tongue."* We can build people up or tear them down simply by the words we choose. Our words have power. Whether or not we realize it, we all have influence. We affect those around us every day, either positively or negatively. Someone is always listening, and as a result, our words help to shape their thoughts.

This even holds true to the words we hear ourselves say. *"I'm sick." "I'm tired." "I'm broke."* Stop it! Be careful that you only speak life! *"I'll never look like her"* (whoever "her" is). *"I can't do it."* **Stop IT!!!** Thinking those negative thoughts is bad enough. Speaking this negativity into your life is downright wrong. You have the power to make a difference, to be a world-changer, to be a mover and a shaker. But you have to know the power of your own voice.

Eleanor Roosevelt said, *"You can never really live anyone else's life, not even your child's. The influence you exert is through your own life, and what you've become yourself."* Think about that. Many of us like to impress the crowd. But God wants us to the impact the individual, starting with ourselves.

Don't underestimate the power of your one voice! I did, and it cost me a lot of years of living in fear. When we consider how much authority and influence we have over others, we should realize the many opportunities we have each and every day to make a difference in someone's life. A smile. A kind word. A simple gesture. Our strongest influence is how we live our own lives. These things matter. By showing love every chance we get, we are offering Christ – every chance we get. It provides us the opportunity to speak up and make the most of the power of that one voice.

Father, thank You for giving us power and influence. Help us to use that power and influence for the good of others and for Your glory. That begins with the words we speak. We are empowered, give us sound minds to exercise and show forth all that You have placed within us. We are Your representatives, and we owe You our best service as we interact with others. We know that we are Your hands and feet. Make our lives examples that others want to emulate. In Jesus' name. Amen.

I SWORE NEVER TO BE SILENT WHENEVER AND WHEREVER HUMAN BEINGS ENDURE SUFFERING AND HUMILIATION. WE MUST ALWAYS TAKE SIDES. NEUTRALITY HELPS THE OPPRESSOR, NEVER THE VICTIM. SILENCE ENCOURAGES THE TORMENTOR, NEVER THE TORMENTED.
Elie Wiesel

Don't Quit
by Anonymous

When things go wrong, as they sometimes will,
When the road you're trudging seems all uphill,
When the funds are low and the debts are high,
And you want to smile, but you have to sigh,
    When care is pressing you down a bit
    Rest if you must, but don't you quit.

Life is queer with its twists and its turns,
    As every one of us sometimes learns,
    And many a failure turns about
When they might have won, had they stuck it out.
    Don't give up though the pace seems slow,
    You may succeed with another blow.

    Often the goal is nearer than,
    It seems to a faint and faltering man,
    Often the struggler has given up
When he might have captured the victor's cup;
And he learned too late when the night came down,
    How close he was to the golden crown.

    Success is failure turned inside out
    The silver tint of the clouds of doubt
    And you never can tell how close you are,
    It may be near when it seems so far;
    So stick to the fight when you're hardest hit,
It's when things seem worst that you must not quit!

SIGNS THAT YOU'RE IN AN ABUSIVE RELATIONSHIP[iii]

YOUR INNER THOUGHTS AND FEELINGS	YOUR PARTNER'S BELITTLING BEHAVIOR
Do you: feel afraid of your partner much of the time?	**Does your partner:** humiliate or yell at you?
avoid certain topics out of fear of angering your partner?	criticize you and put you down?
feel that you can't do anything right for your partner?	treat you so badly that you're embarrassed for your friends or family to see?
believe that you deserve to be hurt or mistreated?	ignore or put down your opinions or accomplishments?
wonder if you're the one who is crazy?	blame you for their own abusive behavior?
feel emotionally numb or helpless?	see you as property or a sex object, rather than as a person?
Your Partner's Violent Behavior or Threats	Your Partner's Controlling Behavior
Does your partner: have a bad and unpredictable temper?	**Does your partner:** act excessively jealous and possessive?
hurt you, or threaten to hurt or kill you?	control where you go or what you do?
threaten to take your children away or harm them?	keep you from seeing your friends or family?
threaten to commit suicide if you leave?	limit your access to money, the phone, or the car?
force you to have sex?	limit your access to money, the phone, or the car?
destroy your belongings?	constantly check up on you?

ADDITIONAL INFORMATION IN AFFIRMING
I HAVE A VOICE!

Physical abuse and domestic violence
When people talk about domestic violence, they are often referring to the physical abuse of a spouse or intimate partner. Physical abuse is the use of physical force against someone in a way that injures or endangers that person. Physical assault or battering is a crime, whether it occurs inside or outside of the family. The police have the power and authority to protect you from physical attack.

Sexual abuse is a form of physical abuse
Any situation in which you are forced to participate in unwanted, unsafe, or degrading sexual activity is sexual abuse. Forced sex, even by a spouse or intimate partner with whom you also have consensual sex, is an act of aggression and violence. Furthermore, people whose partners abuse them physically *and* sexually are at a higher risk of being seriously injured or killed.

It Is Still Abuse If . . . [13]
- **The incidents of physical abuse seem minor** when compared to those you have read about, seen on television or heard other women talk about. There isn't a "better" or "worse" form of physical abuse; you can be severely injured as a result of being pushed, for example.
- **The incidents of physical abuse have only occurred one or two times in the relationship.** Studies indicate that if your spouse/partner has injured you once, it is likely he will continue to physically assault you.
- **The physical assaults stopped when you became passive** and gave up your right to express yourself as you desire, to

---

[13] Source: Breaking the Silence: a Handbook for Victims of Violence in Nebraska

move about freely and see others, and to make decisions. It is not a victory if you have to give up your rights as a person and a partner in exchange for not being assaulted!
- **There has not been any physical violence.** Many women are emotionally and verbally assaulted. This can be as equally frightening and is often more confusing to try to understand.

Economic or financial abuse: A subtle form of emotional abuse

Remember, an abuser's goal is to control you, and he or she will frequently use money to do so. Economic or financial abuse includes:
- Rigidly controlling your finances
- Withholding money or credit cards
- Making you account for every penny you spend
- Withholding basic necessities (food, clothes, medications, shelter)
- Restricting you to an allowance
- Preventing you from working or choosing your own career
- Sabotaging your job (making you miss work, calling constantly)
- Stealing from you or taking your money

Emotional abuse: It's a bigger problem than you think

When people think of domestic abuse, they often picture battered women who have been physically assaulted. But not all abusive relationships involve violence. Just because you're not battered and bruised doesn't mean you're not being abused. Many men and women suffer from emotional abuse, which is no less destructive. Unfortunately, emotional abuse is often minimized or overlooked—even by the person being abused.

Understanding emotional abuse

The aim of emotional abuse is to chip away at your feelings of self-worth and independence. If you're the victim of emotional abuse, you may feel that there is no way out of the relationship or that without your abusive partner you have nothing.

Emotional abuse includes *verbal abuse* such as yelling, name-calling, blaming, and shaming. Isolation, intimidation, and controlling behavior also fall under emotional abuse. Additionally, abusers who use emotional or psychological abuse often throw in threats of physical violence or other repercussions if you don't do what they want.

You may think that physical abuse is far worse than emotional abuse, since physical violence can send you to the hospital and leave you with scars. But, the scars of emotional abuse are very real, and they run deep. In fact, emotional abuse can be just as damaging as physical abuse—sometimes even more so.

Economic or financial abuse: a subtle form of emotional abuse

Remember, an abuser's goal is to control you, and he or she will frequently use money to do so. Economic or financial abuse includes:
- Rigidly controlling your finances
- Withholding money or credit cards
- Making you account for every penny you spend
- Withholding basic necessities (food, clothes, medications, shelter)
- Restricting you to an allowance
- Preventing you from working or choosing your own career
- Sabotaging your job (making you miss work, calling constantly)
- Stealing from you or taking your money

Violent and abusive behavior is the abuser's choice
Despite what many people believe, domestic violence and abuse is not due to the abuser's loss of control over his or her behavior. In fact, abusive behavior and violence is a deliberate choice made by the abuser in order to control you.

Abusers use a variety of tactics to manipulate you and exert their power:
- **Dominance** – Abusive individuals need to feel in charge of the relationship. They will make decisions for you and the family, tell you what to do, and expect you to obey without question. Your abuser may treat you like a servant, child, or even as his or her possession.
- **Humiliation** – An abuser will do everything he or she can to make you feel bad about yourself or defective in some way. After all, if you believe you're worthless and that no one else will want you, you're less likely to leave. Insults, name-calling, shaming, and public put-downs are all weapons of abuse designed to erode your self-esteem and make you feel powerless.
- **Isolation** – In order to increase your dependence on him or her, an abusive partner will cut you off from the outside world. He or she may keep you from seeing family or friends, or even prevent you from going to work or school. You may have to ask permission to do anything, go anywhere, or see anyone.
- **Threats** – Abusers commonly use threats to keep their partners from leaving or to scare them into dropping charges. Your abuser may threaten to hurt or kill you, your children, other family members, or even pets. He or she may also threaten to commit suicide, file false charges against you, or report you to child services.
- **Intimidation** – Your abuser may use a variety of intimidation tactics designed to scare you into submission. Such tactics include making threatening looks or gestures, smashing things in front of you, destroying property,

hurting your pets, or putting weapons on display. The clear message is that if you don't obey, there will be violent consequences.
- **Denial and blame** – Abusers are very good at making excuses for the inexcusable. They will blame their abusive and violent behavior on a bad childhood, a bad day, and even on the victims of their abuse. Your abusive partner may minimize the abuse or deny that it occurred. He or she will commonly shift the responsibility on to you: Somehow, his or her violent and abusive behavior is your fault.

Abusers *are* able to control their behavior – they do it all the time

- **Abusers pick and choose whom to abuse.** They don't insult, threaten, or assault everyone in their life who gives them grief. Usually, they save their abuse for the people closest to them, the ones they claim to love.
- **Abusers carefully choose when and where to abuse.** They control themselves until no one else is around to see their abusive behavior. They may act like everything is fine in public, but lash out instantly as soon as you're alone.
- **Abusers are able to stop their abusive behavior when it benefits them.** Most abusers are not out of control. In fact, they're able to immediately stop their abusive behavior when it's to their advantage to do so (for example, when the police show up or their boss calls).
- **Violent abusers usually direct their blows where they won't show.** Rather than acting out in a mindless rage, many physically violent abusers carefully aim their kicks and punches where the bruises and marks won't show.

The Full Cycle of Domestic Violence: An Example[14]

A man **abuses** his partner. After he hits her, he experiences self-directed **guilt**. He says, "I'm sorry for hurting you." What he does not say is, "Because I might get caught". He then **rationalizes** his behavior by saying that his partner is having an affair with someone. He tells her. "If you weren't such a worthless whore, I wouldn't have to hit you". He then **acts contrite**, reassuring her that he will not hurt her again. He then **fantasizes** and reflects on past abuse and how he will hurt her again. He **plans** on telling her to go to the store to get some groceries. What he withholds from her is that she has a certain amount of time to do the shopping. When she is held up in traffic and is a few minutes late, he feels completely justified in assaulting her because "you're having an affair with the store clerk". He has just **set her up**.

Recognizing the warning signs of domestic violence and abuse

It's impossible to know with certainty what goes on behind closed doors, but there are some telltale signs and symptoms of emotional abuse and domestic violence. If you witness any warning signs of abuse in a friend, family member, or co-worker, take them very seriously.

General warning signs of domestic abuse

People who are being abused may:
- Seem afraid or anxious to please their partner
- Go along with everything their partner says and does
- Check in often with their partner to report where they are and what they're doing
- Receive frequent, harassing phone calls from their partner
- Talk about their partner's temper, jealousy, or possessiveness

---

[14] Source: Mid-Valley Women's Crisis Service

Warning signs of physical violence
People who are being physically abused may:
- Have frequent injuries, with the excuse of "accidents"
- Frequently miss work, school, or social occasions, without explanation
- Dress in clothing designed to hide bruises or scars (e.g. wearing long sleeves in the summer or sunglasses indoors)

Warning signs of isolation
People who are being isolated by their abuser may:
- Be restricted from seeing family and friends
- Rarely go out in public without their partner
- Have limited access to money, credit cards, or the car

The psychological warning signs of abuse
People who are being abused may:
- Have very low self-esteem, even if they used to be confident
- Show major personality changes (e.g. an outgoing person becomes withdrawn)
- Be depressed, anxious, or suicidal

Speak up if you suspect domestic violence or abuse
If you suspect that someone you know is being abused, speak up! If you're hesitating – telling yourself that it's none of your business, you might be wrong, or the person might not want to talk about it – keep in mind that expressing your concern will let the person know that you care and may even save his or her life.

****

WITH THE NEW DAY COMES NEW STRENGTH AND NEW THOUGHTS.
Eleanor Roosevelt

Do's and Don'ts[15]
Do:
- Ask if something is wrong
- Express concern
- Listen and validate
- Offer help
- Support his or her decisions

Don't:
- Wait for him or her to come to you
- Judge or blame
- Pressure him or her
- Give advice
- Place conditions on your support

Talk to the person in private and let him or her know that you're concerned. Point out the things you've noticed that make you worried. Tell the person that you're there, whenever he or she feels ready to talk. Reassure the person that you'll keep whatever is said between the two of you, and let him or her know that you'll help in any way you can.

Remember, abusers are very good at controlling and manipulating their victims. People who have been emotionally abused or battered are depressed, drained, scared, ashamed, and confused. They need help to get out, yet they've often been isolated from their family and friends. By picking up on the warning signs and offering support, you can help them escape an abusive situation and begin healing.

---

[15] Adapted from: NYS Office for the Prevention of Domestic Violence

Next step…
Getting out of an abusive relationship. Do you want to leave an abusive situation, but stay out of fear of what your partner might do? While leaving isn't easy, there are things you can do to protect yourself. You're not alone, and help is available. Read *"Help for Abused and Battered Women"*.

---

[i] Helpguide.org: Domestic Violence and Abuse.
   http://www.helpguide.org/mental/domestic_violence_abuse_types_signs_causes_effects.htm. October 14, 2013.

[ii] All statistics provided were taken from Domestic Violence Statistics:
   http://domesticviolencestatistics.org/domestic-violence-statistics/. October 14, 2013.

[iii] Helpguide.org: Domestic Violence and Abuse.
   http://www.helpguide.org/mental/domestic_violence_abuse_types_signs_causes_effects.htm. October 14, 2013.

****

**FAITH IS SEEING LIGHT WITH YOUR HEART
WHEN ALL YOUR EYES SEE IS DARKNESS.**

****

THERE IS HOPE BECAUSE GOD HAS GIVEN YOU A VOICE WHICH MUST BE HEARD!

www.ingramcontent.com/pod-product-compliance
Lightning Source LLC
Chambersburg PA
CBHW071200090426
42736CB00012B/2405